WIN THEIR HEARTS

WIN Their Minds

SCOTT BRADEN

Published by Dream Chasers Media Group, LLC
Las Vegas, NV
info@dreamchasersmedia.com

Cover Designer: Reneé Fabiano

Library of Congress Control Number: 2010942830
ISBN-13: 978-0-9817581-3-8
ISBN-10: 0-9817581-3-4

Dedication

This book is dedicated to the true heroes of our day—Educators. To Elaina, you are my everything! I love you! Thank you for encouraging me to pen my story of connecting with kids. To Hannah and Micah, you are the two biggest blessings of my life. Thank you for your patience when Daddy was writing. To my students, thank you for allowing me to be a part of your lives. You have taught me so much. And to my colleagues, thank you for believing in me. You have made my life so rich.

Introduction

I'm not an extraordinary person with a long list of accomplishments. I haven't achieved fame or gained great wealth. If you want to know the truth, nothing has ever come easy. Like many of you, I have had to overcome deficits academically, socially, physically and even culturally. I suppose you could say I'm just an ordinary educator, but I do possess something extraordinary. Simply put, I have a passion to connect with young people.

Being a dream maker has become my core passion and purpose. So intense is this passion, it often keeps me awake at night. But, the next day I always find myself rested, restored and ready to begin my day with vigor and enthusiasm because I know that at least one of my students will need me.

I have been in the educational trenches and on the frontlines of students' lives for over twenty years. I have personally taught thousands of students in multiple academic settings, at various levels, and can honestly say that helping young people realize their dreams is something that never grows old.

This book is not a "top ten" list of the best teaching practices or effective pedagogy. Neither is it a philosophical treatise on how best to appropriate rigorous and relevant curriculum, structured collaboration, viable and authentic assessments and/or engagement strategies, even though all of these are necessary and valid for learning to take place.

This book is, however, about connecting with young people and being a dream maker in their lives. It is about empowering harmonious self-systems in the hearts and minds of our students. By "self-system," I'm referring not to the cognitive or meta-cognitive, but to the system within every child that governs how they feel— their "affective domain," with all the unique challenges thereof.

I have always said, and believe more today than ever, that to impact a student's cognitive and meta-cognitive development a teacher must establish an authentic relationship and seize opportunities to win their hearts. I hope that you will find confirmation in this book; confirmation that you can be a vital part of what I believe to be the greatest calling known to man—influencing the formation of young peoples' hearts and minds. It is my hope that as you read, you will find your passion for teaching reinvigorated; that you will discover new approaches to connect with kids and become an effective advocate for them. It is my further hope that when the last page has been read and you close the cover, you will accept the challenge to leave a legacy of greatness for the next generation and dedicate your life to bringing honor to this profession we call "teaching."

If you are presently an educator, I long for this book to engender a rebirth of worth and vitality in your personal life as well as your professional life. I have seen far too many teachers lose their zeal, love and sense of belonging in the classroom. While I'm the first one to admit that being an educator can often be chaotic, mundane, tiresome and unrewarding, I don't believe that it has to be that way. What if there was a way that your career, your mission and your profession could be transformed and energized? What if the mundane could be changed into deeply meaningful experiences and relationships filled with life and vitality? Does this interest you? If so, then read on.

At the beginning of each chapter you'll see reflective quotes titled, "Teacher in the Mirror." The quotes are challenging thoughts, generalizations and ideas intended to motivate and inspire. Let me explain the relevance. Each day, a teacher prepares themselves physically by dressing professionally, and hopefully using proper hygiene. In the same way, "Teacher in the Mirror" is an internal reflection of your self-system. Imagine standing in front of a mirror in a literal sense. The mirror is a true reflection of your physical properties. Now imagine standing in front of the mirror in a figurative sense and having it provoke self-evaluation–an assessment of our self-systems in life and in the classroom. Honest self-evaluation, as frightening as it might be, often demands intervention. Taken seriously, these "Teacher in the Mirror" reflections have the potential to create in you a core desire for purposeful living and purposeful relationships inside and outside of the classroom.

I am a child advocate to the very core. I never tire of hearing success stories and thrill at being a part of these stories. I hope the words written on the pages of this book stimulate your heart and mind as much as they do mine.

My friend, if we want to win the minds of our children, we must first win their hearts. If this is the only concept you take away from this book, then I have successfully passed on to you the greatest of all thoughts. Our young people are longing for you to win their hearts. They need dream makers in their lives, people like you and me, people who will come along side them and uncover the treasure hidden deep within their hearts. May the tireless pursuit of connecting with young people become the motivating force of your life; for if you win the heart of a child, you will be given the opportunity to win their mind.

Table Of Contents

Chapter One
    Legacy 15

Chapter Two
    Dream Maker 25

Chapter Three
    Be A Hero 37

Chapter Four
    Generation 55

Chapter Five
    All About Woo.. 65

Chapter Six
    Never Forget... 93

Chapter Seven
    Find Your Own Calcutta... 107

Chapter Eight
    You Can... 113

Biography.. 119

End Notes.. 121

1

"Legacy"

TEACHER IN THE MIRROR

It was once said to me, "Why would you want to teach history when you could make history?" When you think about it, each and every one of us will make history to some degree. Some life histories will be written into the pages of textbooks. Some life histories will be recorded by men and placed into chronicles. Others will be lost in governmental archives but remembered with legendary magnificence. And yet, all people will etch their personal histories into the hearts and minds of those who surround them, thus, leaving a legacy—good or bad. I'm reminded that empowered educators teach history and make history in the lives of their students every single day!

It seems a fair assumption that all of you have at least one favorite teacher who stands out in your memory. It could be the teacher who used love and understanding to encourage you, or it could be the teacher who used tough love and consequences in the classroom to bring order to your life. Whoever it was, that teacher left an indelible imprint. You were impacted and handed a gift for which you will be eternally grateful. They left you a legacy.

In my opinion, there is no greater calling in life than to influence and mold young peoples' lives. It is honorable indeed! Equal in honor is the teacher who strives to leave a legacy of greatness for his or her students. The father of public education, Horace Mann, once wrote, a"Be ashamed to die until you have won some victory for humanity." To me, winning victories is part of a teacher's legacy. So I ask you, what is the passion that keeps you awake at night? What is the dream that puts a sparkle in your eye, and what is the legacy you long to leave for your students?

There have been two teachers who left legacies of greatness in my life. Although there were many more who made an impact on me, these two touched my life in profound ways—one gave me a love for reading and the other gave me a love for sports, competition and life. The core values that Mrs. "K" and Coach Kelly espoused and modeled, spoke into my adolescent life.

"Reading," Mrs. K would say, "opens up your world to new ideas."

"Can't," Coach Kelly repeated time and time again, "is a word that is foe to ambition."

Both teachers had core values, integrity and conviction unprecedented in my experience and I knew in the depth of my heart that they cared for me as an individual. Both touched my life and both imparted to me their legacies of greatness.

I have had several opportunities to speak to Mrs. K and Coach Kelly over the years. The first occasion for both came many years after graduating high school. In both instances the first thing that came out of my mouth was words that summarized my affection for them and my appreciation of their dream-making in my life.

"Mrs. K...Coach Kelly, I want to honor and thank you for how you have touched my life...for being the molder and shaper of my dreams. I honor you for all that you have done for young people, thank you."

It was exhilarating to see their emotional responses to my sincere words and even more heart-warming to observe their humility and graciousness.

My dear friend and former college roommate, Jon Pritikin, is a motivational speaker today. He, too, had a dream maker teacher who helped him surmount enormous challenges in his life. Over the years, Jon overcame dyslexia and a speech impediment making it nothing shy of a miracle to see him communicate with audiences all over the world today.

It was Jon who I first heard relate a moving testimony of seizing an opportunity to tell his former resource teacher "thank you." I'll never forget when Jon declared to a gathering of students, "Teachers are the molders and shapers of young people's dreams." This phrase became indelibly etched in my mind. Over the years, I have used it in the context of private conversations and while speaking to public audiences, at conventions and in summits. I have used the expression in public documents, in educational curriculum and in private letters. It's as though I can't say or write the word "teacher" without including the phrase "molder and shaper." It still resonates in my heart and mind today.

Please allow me to share a couple of personal stories that reveal how my life was molded and shaped by my high school football coach. The year was 1987 and Coach Kelly was facilitating football practice for the Redwood Ranger football team. I happened to be a wide receiver and in practice I was attempting to run a pattern against my teammate and friend Rudy, a formidable defensive back. Rudy didn't want me to beat his defensive coverage because he'd have to face his position coach—a fate no player wanted to endure. He couldn't stop me with technique or physical skill, so he cheated. Every time I left the line of scrimmage, he would grab my jersey and hold on for dear life!

Unbeknownst to me at the time, Coach Kelly saw the illegal defense but chose not to rebuke Rudy. Instead, Coach Kelly challenged the offense to run the play again. We did, but the play could not be executed accordingly because Rudy repeated his "unsportsmanlike conduct."

"Braden," Coach Kelly screamed, "run the correct route and get separation from Hernandez!"

As I ran back to the huddle, Coach Kelly asked me again, "Why aren't you separating from Hernandez?"

I said, "I can't! He's holding me!"

Yes, my seventeen year old mouth had uttered those ill-famed words and they have been memorialized in my mind ever since.

"Did you say, can't?" The wide-eyed Coach Kelly quickly called me to his side for a private conversation.

I approached humbly, "Coach, Rudy is holding me at the line of scrimmage. I can't get past him."

He grimaced, "Scotty, I know he's holding you; break through it. But, I heard you say the word can't." Coach seized this opportunity to mold and shape my life—not just my football skills.

"Scotty, do you know that can't is a word that is foe to ambition? Essentially, when you say can't, you're really just saying that you won't. Tell yourself that you can! Don't accept failure."

I learned a life lesson that day. I remember being at home later that evening and contemplating the words Coach Kelly had spoken to me: "Can't is a word that is foe to ambition." He was telling me not to accept failure and settle, but to always work through obstacles in my path without justifying or making excuses. Coach Kelly had great wisdom and on that particular day, he seized a golden opportunity to put his arm around my neck, shake me with affection, and teach me a lifelong lesson. He taught me something that has helped make me become the person that I am today. He taught me to never say, "can't."

I have used this nugget of wisdom as a father and have imparted it to my own children. They learned early on to never say the word "can't." In fact, I told them that it was a cuss word and a very bad word to use. On one particular day, when my children were two and four years of age, my daughter seized an opportunity to "mold" and "shape" me, much like Coach Kelly had done so many years before.

My wife and I, along with Hannah and Micah, were driving in the congested traffic of Sacramento, California. We had taken care of some personal business that day and all was quiet on the western front. As I approached a busy intersection, I turned to my navigator (my wife) and said, "Honey, I can't go this way! It's a one way street."

At that moment I heard rumblings from the back seat. It was Hannah.

"Daddy?"

"Yes, Hannah," I responded.

"You can't say that word! Can't is a bad word!"

My wife and I immediately looked at each other and started to laugh.

I replied, "You're right, Hannah. I'm sorry. I should have never have said, can't."

Hannah's words reminded me that I was modeling a world-view for her. It was the literal part of Coach Kelly's figurative lesson on the power of a mindset—the power of a word.

It is crucial to understand that great legacies should transcend generations. Coach Kelly's understanding of the destructive nature of the word "can't" is a legacy that I am leaving for my children and my students. One day, Hannah will walk in the full realization of what I know to be true—the word can't is foe to ambition.

On another occasion, Coach Kelly found out that I wanted to quit the varsity basketball team because I was having problems with the head coach who, in my opinion, was condescending and demeaning. One cold winter day, Coach Kelly spotted me just outside the gymnasium and stopped to ask how things were going in basketball. I revealed my struggles and told him that I was thinking of quitting the team. When he asked me why, I stated that the basketball coach was difficult to play for. Coach paused, shook his head in acknowledgment of my struggles, made a few personal comments, and then spoke so eloquently words of wisdom for which he was known.

"Scotty, you will never be a quitter. Quitters quit and you're not a quitter! Every time you start something, you finish it. Just remember, every time you quit...quitting only gets easier."

To make a long story short, I didn't quit the team. The years have passed, but I still remember Coach's words. Often, I hear him speaking to my own children. How many times have I used his quotes? How many times have I recited his words? Hundreds— perhaps even thousands of times. That is what great teachers do. They mold and they shape—even your very words.

A few years ago, I was hired as an assistant principal at one of the high schools in the community where I was raised. Many of my friends gave me a hard time for taking a job at my alma mater's rival. It was all in fun. Even Coach Kelly gave me a hard time. At a local high school football game, he and I took a few minutes to talk about life, family, and of course, football. It was wonderful. Even as an adult I hung on to every word he spoke and savored every thought his words evoked. The next week, there in my mailbox at work was an envelope from Coach Kelly. It contained a letter to me along with copies of favorite poems and speeches he had saved over the years. His words were as follows:

Scott,

Here are some words that I try to live by every day. I hope you can use them. Keep up the good work. I am proud of what you have done, what you are doing, and who you are. Remember, be a doer not a "tryer."

Coach Kelly

As I sat in my office reading the letter a feeling of joy came over me. I couldn't help but smile, and to be honest...a tear ran down my cheek as I embraced his words of affirmation. I read the last phrase of the letter over and over. Be a doer...not a "tryer." Be a doer...not a "tryer." He was at it again. The old, wise coach had challenged me with a new thought, a new approach, and a new paradigm. Coach Kelly was perpetuating his legacy of greatness. I felt so moved by his words that I sat down and penned the following letter:

Hi Coach!

Just a quick note to say how much I appreciated the words of wisdom you sent my way a few weeks ago. Each article I read exemplified greatness and each article communicated a worldview of which I am very fond. You, of course, have lived the words that were printed on the pages. You have shaped so many young men— including myself. I am forever grateful of your "tough as nails" impartation and the perpetual encouragement and affirmation you gave. It has made me who I am today.

An ancient proverbial truth states that as iron sharpens iron, so one man sharpens another. Coach, thanks for sharpening me into the man I am today and thanks for leaving a legacy of greatness! So many years ago, I heard you say that when you died you wanted to be buried on the fifty-yard line. I know you made the comment in jest, but in a figurative sense, I have not buried you on the fifty-yard line, rather, I have buried you in the core of my being. Coach, you will never die!

Scott

I am reminded that legacy is where your life story lives on. Thus, we must balance our personal lives and our public careers wisely so that our legacies become great. The average lifespan is approximately seventy-five years of age—a statistic worthy of reflection. Life is here today and gone tomorrow. There are only so many opportunities in any given day to spend time with your students and your children, to take your significant other on a romantic getaway or to truly sow into the lives of others. Windows of opportunity are typically limited and rare, so seize these moments today. Breathe fresh life into yourself and the people around you, and you will be on the path to leaving a legacy of greatness.

2

"Dream Maker"

TEACHER IN THE MIRROR

Whether we accept it or not, teachers should be dream makers in the lives of their students. May we never be dream breakers. Our subject is greater than a math formula, greater than an English poem and greater than a scientific experiment. We are dream makers, in the business of helping young people pursue vitality. We cast vision and instill hope for our students. We are success coaches and life coaches helping students appropriate the dreams they were meant to live.

Have you ever thought of yourself as a dream maker? You should. Great teachers are dream makers. Think about this for a moment. What if I gave you the challenge of describing the teaching profession without using the following words: educate, educator, teach or teacher? What if wherever you went, whatever your activities, whenever the question "What do you do for a living?" was posed you would have to answer without the aforementioned words. What would it sound like? What descriptive language would you use to describe your profession?

Consider the following responses. I'm an instructor. I'm a guide. I'm a motivator. I'm a learning facilitator. None of these words and descriptions, in and of themselves, bring enough honor or relevance to the teaching profession. We are so much more than just the social connotations these words convey. Saying the word "teacher" doesn't do justice to our profession, to our mission, or to our passion.

Many times in my life I have been asked what I do for a living. And, most times I have replied, "I'm a teacher." But I must admit, each time I have spoken these words, I have felt as though I didn't give sufficient honor to my profession or to my students. Why? Because I hear the familiar response, "Ohhh, I could never be a teacher!" or because I witness particular facial expressions, body postures or lugubrious intonations that say it all. I'm sure you've seen, heard and experienced the same.

I would like to suggest that the word "teacher" is outdated, abused, misused and misinterpreted. Teachers are so much more than what the word conveys. What if we began calling ourselves "dream makers?" I believe it is a more accurate description of who we are and what we do. It is an empowering word that has been accredited and entrusted to you.

Dream makers are the molders and shapers of young people's lives. Dream makers are experts at significance and belonging. In fact, a dream maker teacher can write a book on the subject and fill it with personal narrative and anecdotes, because they know how to interact and relate with students. They have done it! They facilitate dreams day in and day out. It's not that these dream makers lower their professionalism or standards—in fact they probably have more expectations than the average teacher—but it is that they truly care about their students as individuals. They go out of their way. They extend themselves. They empathize, sympathize, and show compassion. Ultimately, they give to the point of self-sacrifice.

Dream makers go to great lengths to empower a child to feel special, valuable and validated. They will swim oceans and scale mountains to be available to kids. They will go to the ends of the world to help children understand their unique personhood and humanity. They will probe and dig to get a young person to dream, to set goals and to find purpose. They will empower kids to value others as well as themselves.

Ultimately, dream makers act out of compassion and a sense of urgency. Each day, dream makers paint onto the canvasses of kids' minds. They build foundations of confidence, self-actualization and self-esteem. They seize opportunities to instill hope, facilitate vision and mobilize aspiration.

Much has been said about school connection. School connection is the belief by students that adults in school care about their learning and that adults care about them as individuals. The research and data on school connectedness reveals that when young people consistently receive empathy, attention and praise at school, they feel a sense of belonging and support that is the springboard for healthy growth and development.

The research indicates that connected students have a lower rate of absenteeism, fighting, bullying, suicide, drug use and sexual promiscuity. Connected students are more motivated and engaged in learning. These students attend school, complete school and make positive decisions. When kids feel connected at school they are often buffered from the at-risk elements that inhibit their growth and development.

Few would argue with such research and information, but what does connectedness really look like for a dream maker teacher who has a burning desire to win the heart and mind of a child? I will share one such story.

This true story begins in a small California agricultural community of 10,000 people at the base of the pristine Sierra Nevada mountain range. Most of the town's citizens were Mexican-Americans. The average income per family was $23,000 dollars a year. Dilapidated trailers and houses decorated the landscape of this poor community. Gangs ran rampant, teen pregnancy ranked highest in America and hopelessness bred hopelessness in the minds and hearts of its young people.

On a particular spring day, the birds were chirping, the children were in school and the community was at work. All seemed common and mundane, but something was about to happen that would change a young boy's heart.

The boy's name was Jose. He was fourteen years of age. Jose had been born into a poor farm worker's family—a family that was dysfunctional and abusive. There was nothing extraordinary about Jose, but something extraordinary was about to happen to him; something that his teacher would do to win his heart.

The teacher, who Jose called Mr. B, received a puzzling phone call after school one day. This call was from a friend who was a successful businessman.

"Mr. B," the businessman began, "I don't know why, but I feel impressed to send you a chocolate cake in the mail. Do you like chocolate cake?"

"Yes," said Mr. B.

"Will you eat it?"

"Well, probably not," Mr. B replied.

"How come?" The businessman inquired.

"It makes my heart race."

"How about your wife? Does she like chocolate cake?"

"Yes, she does," said Mr. B.

"Will she eat it?"

Mr. B. chuckled, "Probably not, she's on a diet."

The insistent businessman continued, "Well, I'm going to send the cake anyway because I just can't get rid of this feeling that I'm supposed to send you a chocolate cake."

The next day, Jose asked to speak to Mr. B after school. Something was troubling Jose and he needed to talk.

"Mr. B." said Jose, "These past two days have been the worst in my life. Yesterday, it was my fourteenth birthday. The morning started off ok but when I went to school my girlfriend broke up with me and she didn't tell me why. After school, my dad got mad at my sister and ended up beating her up. Then my parents got into a fight and my dad ended up hitting my mom. The police were called to my house and my uncle and aunt ended up getting arrested. Mr. B, nobody said happy birthday to me the entire day. Nobody even bought me a birthday cake."

Jose removed a wristband from his wrist. He showed Mr. B

the cut marks from his lock blade knife. Jose had been cutting himself at night in an attempt to relieve the internal pain and depression he was experiencing. Jose asked Mr. B to promise not to tell anybody.

"Mr. B," said Jose, "I'm so depressed. I don't feel like there is any value to my life."

Mr. B assured Jose that there was purpose and value to his life. He empathized with his loneliness and attempted to verbalize hope for Jose. He reminded Jose that he wasn't alone and offered his personal cell phone number in case he wanted to talk further.

After their conversation, Mr. B headed home. On his way, he called his wife and relayed Jose's story. Mr. B's wife was saddened and offered to host a belated birthday party for Jose the next day. Her intent was to make him a cake and give him a present.

The next day Mr. B hurried to school with a reminder from his wife that she would bring Jose's cake to school around 2:30 pm so the students could celebrate and honor Jose's late birthday.

At lunchtime, Mr. B received a phone call from his wife.

"You won't believe it!" she said. "I was just getting ready to bake Jose's cake when a Federal Express truck dropped off a large box on the porch. In it was a beautiful chocolate cake preserved by dry ice. It is absolutely gorgeous! I've never seen anything like it before."

Mrs. B drove the chocolate cake to school at the prearranged time. Mr. B couldn't wait to see this cake! When the last period of the day arrived, Jose walked into Mr. B's class and sat in his assigned corner seat. Unbeknownst to the students, Mr. B had the cake covered and in the front of the classroom. Jose had no idea what was about to unfold in his life.

Mr. B started the class with his usual greeting, "Good afternoon class."

"Good afternoon, Mr. B," they replied in unison.

"I want to start off by telling you a true story," said Mr. B. "Once upon a time there was a little Hispanic baby boy who was born to proud Hispanic parents. Every birthday they would celebrate his birth with festivities, piñatas and a birthday cake. But on one particular birthday, his fourteenth as a matter of fact, everything went crazy. His whole world was turned upside down. His family got into a fight and they forgot this little boy's birthday. Everything seemed to go wrong on the night they were supposed to celebrate his birth. In fact, not one person in his family, not even his friends said 'Happy Birthday' to him. They didn't even give him a birthday cake."

"Just three days ago, I got a call from a very wealthy friend. He told me that he felt impressed to send me a chocolate cake. At the time, I had no idea why he was sending me a cake, but now I do. You're probably wondering what this has to do with the boy who had a terrible birthday. Well, today, this boy is in our class and the birthday cake has been delivered especially for him."

The students began to cheer.

Mr. B shouted over the cheering, "Everyone, this boy is your classmate, Jose!" He continued, "Jose, we're throwing a party in your name and in your honor. I've brought forks and plates, napkins and cups—I even have a special present for you."

Tears of joy trickled down Jose's cheeks.

Mr. B said, "Students, this isn't an ordinary birthday cake.

This cake has been hand crafted with intricate detail. It's not a Costco or a Walmart cake. This cake is not a ten-dollar cake or a fifty-dollar cake. This is a gourmet cake from the East Coast and it is very expensive. But, in my book, this cake is priceless because it was handmade for Jose."

Mr. B had the cake underneath a box and he was holding the exterior of the box, preparing to lift the top, when he made one last statement. "Students, when I show you this cake, you won't even recognize it as a cake. Rather, it looks like a wrapped birthday gift with a flamboyant bow on top. In just a second you will see the most brilliant colors shine forth. In all my life, I have never seen a more beautiful cake. Jose, let it be known for all of time that this cake represents your inward beauty."

When Mr. B lifted the box off the top of the cake the students let out a roar of astonishment.

"Oh my goodness," said some.

"It's beautiful," exclaimed others.

"You're so lucky, Jose," stated another.

Mr. B then led the class in singing happy birthday to Jose. The cake was cut, the present was opened and Jose's heart was won. At the end of class, Jose hung around to talk to Mr. B. The other students had gone and just the two of them were left, just the way that Jose wanted it.

"Mr. B," Jose began, "This was the nicest thing that anybody has ever done for me. I will remember this for the rest of my life." He gave Mr. B a gigantic hug and with tears streaming down his cheeks and his voice weakened from emotion, Jose said one last time, "Thank you, Mr. B, thank you."

The years have come and the years have gone. Jose went on to college, started a career and Mr. B...well, he still works with kids. The one thing Mr. B knows for certain—if you win the hearts of young people, you just might be given the opportunity to win their minds.

Not every teacher is a dream maker. In fact, many people hear the word "teacher" and immediately thoughts and images of a dream breaker surfaces. We have all known those teachers to whom this term could truthfully be applied. Unfortunately, there have been far too many dream breakers involved in the lives of young people.

Dream breakers negatively impact their students in word and deed, and sadly, students tend to remember them even if they had five empowering teachers. Dream breakers give education a bad name and provide yet another reason for negative views of this honorable profession.

It's depressing to us all when we hear the horror stories of dream breaking teachers. In all honesty, I think that every teacher, knowingly or unknowingly, has at times been an unwilling dream breaker. Teachers are fallible and imperfect—even with the purest of intentions. Teachers are asked to do so much and in such short time. They are always in the trenches and on the front lines of their students' problems. They are always on the stage of public performance, responsibility, professional growth, assessment, evaluation, collaboration and the list goes on.

In a figurative way, teachers live their lives as a fish in a fish tank—always looked at, always judged and always struggling to be heard. Every day, teachers are subject to the demands of students, parents, school districts, school boards, and educational stakeholders. The ever-present anxieties and burdens are pervasive and it is difficult for a teacher to be selfless in such a demanding occupation.

To add fuel to the fire, students today are needy, anxious and consumed with themselves. Administrators are all too often direct, demanding and evaluative. Districts employ burdensome programs, insufficient paradigm shifts and inadequate personnel. School boards are politically motivated and exasperating. Let's face it... bureaucracy exasperates us all! And yet, dream makers stand up to every challenge and obstacle intent on winning the hearts of their students so that one day they can influence their minds.

One of the most dynamic components of being a dream making teacher is encouraging students to dream—and to dream big. Many kids today live in "survival mode," just hoping to have basic needs met. They have been so beaten down that they are afraid to dream. The dream maker teacher has the power to tap into dreams—regardless of how deeply under fear and past failure these dreams may be buried—and to enable students to unleash their full potential. How beautiful are the steps of one who opens a student's heart, allowing dreams to run free.

I heard a speaker many years ago speak about the life of Martin Luther King Junior. It moved me—not because of who MLK was and the honorable life he lived—but because of the dream makers in MLK's life and how they impressed him to dream. The story I heard went something like this:

The year was 1944. The setting was Morehouse College in Atlanta, Georgia. On this hot, sweltering summer day, Morehouse

College president, Dr. Benjamin Elijah Mays sat at his desk doing what everyone else was trying to do...just trying to stay cool, when he heard a knock on his office door.

"Come in!" he said. The big, wooden door swung open and in the doorway stood a gentleman and his teenage son. Dr. Mays excitedly jumped to his feet and grabbed the hand of his visitor.

"Come on in my friend." The man was Martin Luther King, Sr., the father of historical civil rights leader, Martin Luther King, Jr. Both Senior and Junior stepped into the president's office.

Once they were all seated, MLK Sr. began to talk. "I know you're busy, so I won't take much of your time. I just wanted to introduce you to my son, Marty. Marty is fifteen years old and he just graduated from high school. He will be coming to Morehouse College in the fall." Senior paused as if in appraisal of his son, before continuing.

"He's a good boy with good moral character. More than that, though, I believe he's got something in him that can really make a difference. In fact, I'm sure of it. But, he's missing one thing, Dr. Mays...just one thing. I brought him here today to ask a favor of you."

He paused and Dr. Mays gestured for him to continue.

"I'm not looking for tuition—that's already taken care of. I don't want room and board either. It's bigger than that." Piercing Dr. Mays with a level gaze he said passionately, "I'm asking you to teach my boy how to dream."

Without a word, Dr. Mays stood and went to the side of his office where he grabbed a piece of paper and handed it to MLK Jr.

"Read this, Marty! Read it every day and it will change your life."

Martin Luther King Jr. did just that.

The words on that small piece of paper have been inscribed in the Benjamin Mays National Memorial that stands on the campus of Morehouse College.

"It must be borne in mind that the tragedy in life doesn't lie in not reaching your goal. The tragedy lies in having no goal to reach. It isn't a calamity to die with dreams unfulfilled, but it is a calamity not to dream. It is not a disaster to be unable to capture your ideal, but it is a disaster to have no ideal to capture. It is not a disgrace not to reach the stars, but it is a disgrace to have no stars to reach for. Not failure, but low aim is sin."

Dr. Mays and Martin Luther King, Sr. were dream makers in the life of the young Martin Luther King. They empowered and encouraged him to dream big and today we recognize Dr. King's "I Have A Dream," as the speech that defined the Civil Rights Movement.

I have learned in life that dreams become reality because dream makers have influenced dreamers. So the next time you're asked what you do for a living, simply respond, "I'm a dream maker!"

3

"Be A Hero"

TEACHER IN THE MIRROR

A hero is not just someone who has a red cape, wears an "S" on his chest and muscles his way through steel buildings. A hero is one who puts everything aside to help someone in need. Our students need heroes! They need common people doing uncommon acts. Henry Ford once said, "There is no man living who isn't capable of doing more than he thinks he can do." Be a hero and teach your students to be heroes in the lives of others.

There's something special about everyday heroes. They come in all shapes and sizes. For Kristi, Cory became her hero and he was only five years old. No, he didn't pack a powerful punch, he didn't even come to the rescue with flashes of lightening or sizzling speed—but he did destroy the villain attempting to overtake Kristi. How was it that a five-year-old boy became a hero to his sixteen-year-old sister?

Kristi always struggled to believe that she was special and valuable. She felt abandoned by her biological father. She never truly saw the love that her mother and others showed her because she was trapped by a lie that said she was not important. Her parent's bitter divorce and the destructive relationship that resulted between Kristi and her father left the young girl feeling utterly alone. Although she knew that her mother loved her, she longed for the acceptance and approval of her father.

A few years after the divorce, her mother married an honorable man. He, like her mother, cherished Kristi. He attempted to bring value to her life in everything that he did, but she dismissed his love. Shortly after this marriage, Kristi's mother gave birth to her two siblings—a sister and a brother. These children adored their big sister—she could do no wrong in their eyes. Kristi continued to struggle with her feelings of worthlessness; she never felt as though she was part of the family and nothing they did could penetrate her wounded heart. She dismissed their affection, their adoration and their kindness on her quest for her biological father's approval.

She was convinced that she fell short of her biological father's expectations. Nothing seemed to please him. In all honesty, and to her dismay, her father exemplified a cold and calloused disposition towards everyone. A life of compromise and chaos had so hardened him that he didn't know how to love his own family. But Kristi's mom, stepfather and siblings never stopped reaching out to her. They were real, transparent and full of life. Even to the most casual observers, Kristi's family was fun, healthy and caring.

On a particular cold, wintry day, Kristi approached her mother with a proposition. She shared with her mother that she wanted to live with her biological father. This devastated her mother who had always feared that Kristi would see this as a plausible solution to her inner struggles.

"How could she?" Her mother thought, "How could she do this to herself? Doesn't she know that seeking the approval of her father is a vain attempt—a hopeless chase?"

Recently, Kristi's mom had observed Kristi frequently hiding herself away in the bedroom in an attempt to detach physically and emotionally from the family. It was as though Kristi was purposely sabotaging anything honorable or virtuous in her life. Acts of kindness by her siblings had been dismissed. Words of affection were discarded. Day after day, Kristi made damaging choices in school and relationships. The villains of depression and loneliness increased...and ultimately, nobody could change Kristi's mind. So, Kristi's wise and loving mom responded to Kristi's request to leave.

"Honey," she said, "The choice is yours to make. I will support you and honor you but I want you to know how much this family will miss you. We love you!"

The night before Kristi was to move, little Cory approached his big sister in the living room.

"KK," he said, for KK was what Cory had always called Kristi.

"KK, I made a card for you." Kristi looked at the card perplexed. A lot of time and effort had obviously gone into the making of this card. It had been hand crafted with a specific intent. The card was folded in two. On one side was the stick-figure picture of a little boy wearing a baseball cap and holding hands with his older sister. A childish hand had drawn tears streaming down the brother's cheeks. On the other side of the card were the words: *KK,*

I love you! I love you! I love you! We love you! I will think about you all day long and all night long. Love, Cory.

Tears now filled KK's eyes. This humble card had penetrated her calloused heart. An epiphany of love had occurred for Kristi. Her mother stood in the kitchen, observing her daughter in the living room. Kristi's hands covered her face as the tears streamed down her cheeks. She sat the card down on the table and then picked it up over and over again, as she struggled to regain her composure.

This scene continued even after Cory left the room. A speechless KK stared at the card, then looked away, only to have her attention drawn back to the sweet offering from her brother.

After ten minutes...it happened! What happened, you ask? You know...the thing that KK needed to happen; something that we all need to happen at various times in our lives—the "something" that corrects our distortions. Kristi needed a hero in her life, and that is exactly what she got. Cory had shown up at precisely the right time, with precisely the right words and precisely the right motivation. Cory was her hero!

Kristi's mother watched KK get up from the couch and walk gingerly into Cory's room. She approached Cory who was on his bed playing with toys.

"Cory," she stifled a sob, "Thank you so much for my card. I love you." After she spent a few more moments hugging and thanking Cory, Kristi approached her mother in the kitchen.

"Mom, I have something to show you," she said. Kristi handed the card to her mother, who read it and began to cry. Kristi reached out to embrace her mother.

"Mom, I think I know where my home is. Would it be alright if I unpacked my things and put them back in my bedroom where they belong?" Kristi's mother wrapped her in arms of love as they cried tears of joy together.

Cory's heroic action rescued Kristi in the midst of her emotional crisis. He brought value to Kristi, which is exactly what heroes do. They ask themselves—what is it that I can do to help the person I care about overcome a particular obstacle?

Little Cory had learned in kindergarten that kindness, listening, sharing, asking first, taking turns and playing fair are all valuable life-skills necessary for civility and coexistence. But Cory's action that day reminds us that he had also learned something far beyond his maturity level; something much more empowering. In reaching out to his beloved sister, he had learned how to be a hero in the life of another human being.

As teachers, we are uniquely positioned to be the greatest heroes on the face of the earth. Each day, students figuratively sit at our feet, but often it seems that we have forgotten (or never truly learned) how to be heroes in their lives.

Cory reminds us that heroes transcend age, sex, education and status. "Hero" is not a position or an occupation, nor is it status or social reputation. A true hero is simply a human being who puts everything aside to help someone in need. A true hero comes to the rescue, with the right actions and the right words at the right moment. A true hero is willing to sacrifice time, talent and treasure to help the hurting and needy.

Although they perform extraordinary and praiseworthy deeds, there is no mystique to the role of being a true hero. Our culture is quick to honor athletes, movie stars and singers for their endeavors, heroic or not, but slow to honor teachers. May I declare that this needs to change!

People tend to see themselves as they are seen. And sadly, teachers have often seen themselves the way society perceives them as "only a teacher." Many teachers have forgotten that the nature of their mission (job) entails being a hero and a dream maker. Teachers don't have to come to the rescue, but they choose to because they want to be the hero that their students need. There is no legal requirement or professional responsibility that demands intervention; teachers just respond. They don't seek to justify and rationalize; they just react. Heroic teachers march into the frontlines of children in need, choosing not to retreat or hide behind other obligations.

Each day I watch for opportunities to be a hero in the life of a student. Like Cory, I look for the right moment, the right word and the right act, in order to fashion the right rescue for the right student. Several years ago, I had the opportunity to be a hero in the life of my student, Pedro.

Having immigrated illegally to the USA from Mexico just three years prior, I was amazed at Pedro's knowledge of the English language. He was brilliant, articulate and possessed charm, personality and leadership skills. Pedro never had a frown on his face and students were drawn to his kindness and humor and he was always appreciative of the friends and teachers he had in his life. In fact, each day as Pedro left my class he would say, "Thank you for teaching us, Mr. Braden. Have a great day."

I always responded, "My honor, Pedro. You have a great day as well."

Two years after having Pedro as a student I received an unusual phone call. It was in the middle of winter vacation and I was at home. My cell phone rang and I answered. Cindy—the principal's secretary began to speak.

"Mr. Braden," she said, "Pedro Martinez is here in the office. He was asking for your phone number but I didn't want to give it out so I'm calling you instead. Pedro would like to speak to you. Would you like to speak to him?"

"You bet! Let me talk to Pedro," I said.

Pedro was on the other line.

"Hi Pedro! How are you?" I thought he was calling because he wanted to talk and shoot the breeze. These types of calls are not uncommon from my former students—and knowing the impoverished life style Pedro was accustomed to—I wouldn't have put it past him to use the school's phone.

"Mr. Braden," he said. "My family is in a really bad situation. I need to talk to you."

My heart sank, "Absolutely! What's up?" I knew something serious was troubling Pedro.

"I don't know if you know this, but I'm living with my sister, her husband and their two kids. My mom is in Mexico. Anyways, my family was on their way to moving up to Washington so we could pick apples but my little niece got sick and we never made it to Washington. We had to rush my niece to the hospital. She's still in the hospital. We thought she was going to die, but she's doing better right now. We stayed in a hotel room while we waited to see what was wrong with my niece. But, my brother-in-law wasn't able to work so we had to bring the moving van and all our stuff back to town."

"Is your niece ok, Pedro?" I interrupted.

"We don't know. The doctors don't know for sure what the problem is."

"So your niece is still in the hospital?" I asked.

"Yes."

"How is your family handling this?"

"They're really sad, Mr. Braden. We decided to come back to town because we don't have anywhere to go and my brother-in-law is running out of money."

"I'm so sorry, Pedro."

"Mr. Braden, my family doesn't know what to do. I told them that we have to talk to you. I told my sister that my teacher always told me that he would be there for me if I needed him; that you always said that there are people in your life for a reason. I told my sister that there's one person I could trust—and that's you."

I didn't know if Pedro was practicing being a cunning used car salesman or if Pedro was being legitimate, but at that moment, I didn't care. I've always told my students that I would be there for them—especially in crisis situations. Although there have been times that I've failed to be a hero in the lives of my students, I wasn't going to fail this time.

"Pedro, I appreciate your words. How can I help you?"

"Mr. Braden, I feel terrible even asking this of you. But I over-heard my sister and brother-in-law say that they needed a deposit to rent a house."

"Pedro is trying to fix his family's problems," I thought to my-self as Pedro was talking. "Here is a young man taking the bull by the horns in an attempt to bring peace to his family—what an honorable young man!"

Pedro continued, "Maybe you can talk to somebody that can help us out?"

"Pedro," I said, "Meet me at Taco Bell in one hour. Can you bring your family?"

"Yes, I appreciate it, Mr. Braden."

I got off the phone and related the story to my wife. "What are you going to do?" she asked.

"I know we don't have much in our savings, but would it be alright if I gave them some money?"

My wife looked at me with love and admiration, "Scott, give them the rest of our savings. They need it more than we do."

So off I went. At the bank, I pulled out one thousand dollars, leaving only a few cents in the account, then quickly rushed to the parking lot of Taco Bell. Soon a small U-Haul truck pulled up and out jumped Pedro from the driver's side. His brother-in-law and sister also got out. Pedro walked over and gave me a hug, then I shook his family's hands and made small talk with Pedro acting as translator.

"Well," I started, "I know you're in a very challenging time in your life right now so I want to give you a gift. I'm not a wealthy man, I'm just an ordinary person but I want to give you what's left of my savings account. This is money that I have saved for my children but I want to give it to you and your children. Please accept this gift, I hope it can help you get back on your feet."

Pedro's family began to cry as Pedro translated his brother-in-law's words, "We will pay this money back to you as soon as we can."

"Not necessary," I said, "I have given it as a gift, it is yours and there are no strings attached. However, if you want to bring honor to your family, do the same thing I've done for you. In the future, when you're back on your feet and you're able to save some money, be a hero in the life of somebody else who needs your help."

Pedro and his family were in disbelief and I was humbled and honored to have been part of this much-needed rescue. We went our separate ways, and eventually they did get back on their feet.

One more thing...the thousand-dollar investment, well, check this out: Two weeks after giving Pedro and his family the money, my wife got a phone call from a friend who she helps with a non-profit. He wanted to give her a two thousand dollar check for all her hard work and dedication to his organization. Look at that! Give a thousand dollars and get two thousand in return. Not a bad investment!

There really is no better feeling then knowing that you have been a hero to someone in need. One could say that being a hero gives birth to being a hero; it champions and perpetuates goodness. Being a hero is contagious and when teachers catch hold of this concept—it changes their attitude and brings newfound vigor to their respective missions.

Mr. Delgado sat in my office—disgusted. Those disrespectful freshman students were at it again. It was the third week of a new semester and tardiness to class was wearing on him. A twenty-five year veteran of public education, it seemed as though Mr. Delgado was just "doing his time." At least it seemed that way until one conversation—a "be a hero" conversation.

Mr. Delgado adhered to the philosophy that you had to make a student feel bad in order to make them do better. Many teachers appropriate this philosophy into their class management repertoire and many times I have seen teachers "rip" into students for inappropriate behavior. Ivory was one such student for Mr. Delgado. Ivory was perpetually tardy to his class and her behavior exasperated Mr. Delgado. His firm talks outside of the classroom had little impact on her. Nonchalant, insubordinate responses to his directives manifested every time he attempted to actuate change, and his Spanish blood boiled each time Ivory defied him.

Mr. Delgado had been raised in Spain. He was a handsome, charismatic and distinguished gentleman; perhaps a bit macho and innocently chauvinistic. Having been raised by a firm and stoic father—a police officer in a large Spanish city—Mr. Delgado was disciplined and consequently tough on students. He was not about to let Ivory get the best of him or his class with her perpetual tardiness.

"Principal Braden, You need to do something with Ivory!" he said. Very rarely did Mr. Delgado bring a student to me, because he was well able to handle most of his pupil challenges.

"What did she do?" I asked.

Mr. Delgado proceeded to recount Ivory's many improprieties. After I heard him out, I explained to him some of the challenges Ivory had been dealing with in her life. Not for the sake of justification, but in an endeavor to bring understanding. I had been working with the family for over a year and if any child had been dealt a bad hand in life—Ivory was that child. Her father had been sentenced to life in prison. Her mother had just been released from jail and was attempting to better herself. Ivory had been molested as a little girl, recently raped, and had spent a good deal of time in and out of foster care. She was a confused teenager who struggled with her identity and her sexuality. Further complicating her life was her affiliation with the *Nortena* gang. Was it any wonder that anger raged in her heart?

Mr. Delgado sat stunned as I related these details of Ivory's life. "Wow," he said, "I didn't have any idea."

"Mr. Delgado," I continued, "I bet if you approached Ivory with tenderness and attempted to be a hero in her life, she would respond positively to you and your classroom procedures. She tries to be tough on the outside but when she sees tenderness she melts."

I continued my speech on being a hero in the life of students rather than being autocratic, even at the risk of offending my colleague and friend. Although Mr. Delgado respectfully listened, I knew he resisted my words as evidenced by his occasional rebuttals cloaked in cynicism and negativity. Ultimately, he agreed that he would give "being a hero" a shot.

The following day, I was at my desk when Mr. Delgado walked in with a smile on his face. For the next five minutes, he proceeded to tell me about the conversation that he and Ivory had earlier in the day. He had approached her with sensitivity for the first time, and for the first time their conversation had been quite successful. He told her that he didn't know much of her personal story but he could guess that her life was difficult. He assured her that he didn't want to add to her difficulties, he just wanted to be there for her.

His words had melted her heart. Mr. Delgado sat in disbelief as he watched tears stream down Ivory's cheeks and he witnessed her disposition change from one of resistance to one of amiability.

The next day, I happened to see Ivory's mother on campus and we spoke. Through the course of our conversation she let me know how appreciative she was of Mr. Delgado. She said that her daughter had come home after school the day before excitedly talking about a teacher on campus named Mr. Delgado. Ivory conveyed to her mother that Mr. Delgado understood her, and was convinced that he was the type of teacher that she could open up to. As Ivory's mom continued to speak, all I could do was smile, smile and smile some more. Mr. Delgado had indeed become a hero to Ivory and to her mother.

Not only do teachers need to be heroes in the lives of their students, they need to teach their students to be heroes in the lives of each other. We must teach and model how to protect one another, how to brag about one another's strengths and how to defend one another's weaknesses. Young people need to learn how noble it is to rescue and protect those who have been abandoned, dejected, rejected and physically or emotionally wounded. They need to learn why the risk of failure and embarrassment is not too steep a price to pay to do what is honorable.

I read some staggering statistics recently. According to [b]Dr. Spencer Kagan, 160,000 students skip school each day because they fear bullies. More than one in three students report that they do not feel safe at school. Eighty-three percent of girls and sixty percent of boys have been sexually harassed at school (touched, pinched, or grabbed in a sexual way).

Our schools should be a safe haven that respects the individual student, and yet bullying in America is all too prevalent. Again, educators must teach their students how to be heroes in the lives of one another.

In his annual state of education address, California state schools' superintendent ᶜJack O'Connell, called for adding "character-building" to school curricula. He stated that many of the schools that have been most successful at closing achievement gaps, have high standards for civility, and encourage students to be active in their communities. This doesn't surprise me.

When we empower young people to give their lives away and not hold on to what they can't keep, we are ultimately giving them happiness. I often communicate to my students that the greatest in society are those who help the helpless and that the happiest people in America are those who give their lives for a noble purpose. Students need to know that their heroic efforts may not be noticed now, but they will be noticed in the future. Teaching your students character and exhorting them to employ core values is paramount to education.

I have shared the following story with teens in dozens of school assemblies. It is my personal experience as a teenage boy, attempting to be a hero in the life of my childhood classmate, Pete.

I knew Pete from the time that I was six years old. We went to the same elementary school, junior high and senior high. We knew the same people and resided in the same neighborhood, but lived very different lives. The kids at school called Pete a nerd. In the third grade he soiled himself in class while sitting at his desk. The kids never let him hear the end of it.

In the fifth grade Pete had a reputation for picking his nose and eating his boogers, and to be honest, I even observed him doing this his freshman year of high school. Pete's clothes never matched, his hair was always messy and students stayed as far away as possible. Sad to say, he was an untouchable; he felt unlovable.

But unlike most of us, Pete was extremely bright. He was an avid reader with various intellectual pursuits and a wide range of interests. Pete loved history, science, sports and trivia. He loved learning and never hesitated to speak up in class. When we were in elementary school this was annoying, but in high school the students were entertained.

Pete and I had Civics together our senior year, and I always enjoyed the discourse Pete would have with the teacher. Pete was a great conversationalist, but his shallow and immature peers would not accept him. I'll never forget the day that our Civics' teacher taught us an ancient Chinese proverb that says, "If you want to understand people, you must walk a mile in their shoes." I remember thinking about the proverb, even after class was out...and then *it* occurred. What occurred? The most demoralizing event any student would have to undergo. Matt, a varsity football player, publically subjected Pete to extreme humiliation. Matt kicked some books that Pete had dropped from his locker, and as Pete leaned down to retrieve the books, Matt added insult to injury by kicking them again, this time out of Pete's hands. The students around Pete's locker watched the incident and began to laugh. Pete wasn't laughing. His head was down. He was demoralized and he didn't dare look up at the aggressor.

As Matt left, I approached Pete and asked him if he needed some help. He refused to answer me—probably thinking that I would do the same thing Matt had just done. I remember walking away that day asking myself what it would be like to be Pete. I was upset that Matt had done such a thing and I made a promise to myself that I would try to reach out to Pete to let him know that not all jocks harass and intimidate innocent people.

Pete and I had two very different social journeys. I never knew what it meant to be bullied, teased or the object of ridicule, but Pete did. Pete never knew what it meant to hit home runs, score touchdowns and have people cheer and scream your name, but I did. Pete never knew what it meant to be accepted and respected, even looked up to by his peers, but he deserved it. He was an easygoing kid—a sweet kid. I just wanted to show Pete that he mattered and that I accepted who he was.

The next day at school, as I was walking from one class to another, I saw Pete and began to walk with him. At first, he was very reserved and uncommunicative. He had little trust for me, but through the course of the year, Pete and I walked and talked together on various occasions. We talked about professional football, World War II, college, family and a host of other topics teenage boys find interesting. In short, Pete and I became friends.

The last time I saw Pete was graduation night. I remember watching him walk across the stage and visiting with his family after the ceremonies. That year, I had walked a mile in his shoes and had attempted to bring honor to my friend, Pete. Others knew him to be a nerd, but I knew him to be unique, brilliant, kind and friendly.

Twenty years came and went. I had not heard from Pete until one spring day while driving in Northern California. On my way to an appointment, I took a detour down a side road. In the process, I noticed a distinguished gentleman that resembled my old friend Pete. I slowed down, almost to a complete halt—it was Pete! I put my foot on the brake, rolled down my window, and started to holler his name. Just at that moment a car sped past me on the left side, horn honking to let me know that I was in error. The driver even displayed his middle finger to tell me that I was number one. But it didn't matter to me, I yelled Pete's name as loudly as I could and waited for his response. Sure enough, he waved, but I knew that he didn't recognize the stranger yelling his name. I pulled my truck to the side of the road and jumped out. As I ran across the street I noticed that Pete's appearance had changed substantially. He had aged gracefully, and I couldn't help but notice how dignified he looked.

"Pete, Pete, it's me—Scott Braden."

"Scott Braden...how are you?"

I gave Pete a big hug, patted his arms and said, "It's been twenty years my friend. What are you up to these days?"

"Well, I'm a university professor."

My heart soared. If only the high school crowd could see him today, I thought to myself. Pete had made it! He had made it despite the negativity he had dealt with in adolescence.

For the next few minutes Pete and I caught up on each other's life journeys. We talked about family, children and goals.

At the end of our conversation, I looked him in the eyes and said with some reservation, "Pete, I will never forget the day that Matt..."

Pete raised his hand to silence me. "I remember that day, Scott."

He knew what I was going to say and it was as if he had waited twenty years for the opportunity to tell me what he was about to communicate.

He paused for a second, put his head down and began, "Scott, I can honestly say that you were the only jock in high school that treated me with respect."

I was overcome with emotion as he expressed his heart to me and I was awed by his memory of the details of our conversations.

"Well, my friend, the teenage crowd always overlooked the person you were. It doesn't surprise me in the least that you're a professor today and doing what you do. I'm proud of the person you were and I'm proud of the person you are."

As we parted company that day, I drove away with a sense of honor and nostalgia. Pete was still part of my life.

When I tell students the Pete story, I challenge them to be a hero in the lives of each other. I challenge and exhort them to stand up for each other and honor one another. I let them know of the many ways that they can give, serve, protect, befriend and sacrifice. As educators, we need to continually paint a picture of our students as heroes to one another.

There are many schools employing character and life-skills based programs today and they are to be commended. I hope that one day soon *Be A Hero* campaigns will be so powerful and wide spread that many precious lives would be impacted by such advocacy. May we always raise *Be A Hero* awareness to our students for there is value in every child.

4

"Generation"

TEACHER IN THE MIRROR

Teens today live in a restless culture—the antithesis of a harmonious self-system. The word "restless" is defined as antsy, unable to relax or be still, a constant fretful stamping of hooves and or an itch for excitement. Gentle and humble educators have the power to provide "rest" for an anxious generation of young people.

Not too long ago a close friend of mine was having a conversation with a famous baseball player. At one point the ball player said, "When I swing and hit a home run, everybody cheers, but, when I swing and strike out everybody boos."

My friend suggested, "You can't live to please the crowd, for if you do, you will always be at the mercy of the crowd."

What a great metaphor for this generation of young people. It's as though they are living their lives to please the crowd. One minute they're accepted, the next minute they're rejected. As educators, we're attempting to empower young people to rise above the crowd and find their value from the moral center of their being. It's a hard sell, for deeply ingrained inside most young people is the nearly unshakable resolve that their value and self-worth is based upon the crowd's acceptance.

I have seen major newspapers and periodicals identify this generation of young people as a barbaric generation; a tuned-out generation; a generation of animals; an unromantic generation; a chaotic generation. There is little debate that the levels of egregious behavior observed in teens has escalated as never before in history, but the labels and generalizations are inappropriate, demeaning and unjust.

The *Mosaic Generation*, as they have been coined, live eclectic and stressful lifestyles with non-linear thinking patterns. Rather than using logic they embrace contradictions. Their friendships are always in a state of flux. They are fueled by technology and are morally pragmatic without being particularly dogmatic. The consensus among educators is that this confused generation is difficult to influence.

A young man named Brennan was brought into my office for a behavioral infraction. He had stolen a stack of hall passes and forged an attendance clerk's signature with the intention of getting his girlfriend out of class.

Brennan was a fun loving, intelligent young man with a beautiful smile. He and I had spent a lot of time together during which he had opened up to me about his life. The year before, he had been living in a car with his drug-addicted mother. With his father incarcerated, Brennan became the de facto patriarch of the family, doing everything a fifteen year-old could do to keep his mother and younger siblings together and to provide much needed stability.

In addition to his family's troubles and challenges, Brennan was playing football, getting good grades and even maintaining a relationship with a girlfriend. He worked side jobs to contribute to the family coffers and tried to keep the pain and chaos of their mother from his siblings. He was a unique young man...an outstanding individual.

But over the course of the year, something drastically changed in Brennan. His smile was replaced with pain, and anger filled his heart. His once kind and wise words vanished along with his good grades. Brennan was no longer living, but merely existing.

He sat there in front of me, dejected, humiliated and distant. I sat across from him feeling compassion but also saddened and burdened at the change in my young friend.

"Brennan, I don't want to talk about the hall pass incident right now. I want to talk about you, because I care about you. What happened to the old Brennan?"

"What do you mean, Mr. Braden?" came his emotionless response.

For the next twenty minutes, I was able to engage Brennan in probably the most meaningful conversation of his life. Here he was, in a crisis situation, and a vice principal was talking to him as a father would a son. At the end of our time together, discipline was issued and willingly accepted by Brennan, but the real value of that day was contained in the words I shared; words that allowed the walls of his heart to be breached so that open and honest communication could take place.

We talked about trust, forgiveness, purpose and hope. Brennan, like many of his generation, expressed that he had a hard time trusting anyone. I have heard this from the mouths of teenagers time and time again. I can't even begin to explain the magnitude of distrust in young people today. I have heard it said, and I believe it to be true, that trustworthiness is the number one character trait that teenagers value in others. They want to trust those in authority, they want to trust their family and they want to trust their friends. And yet, it is extremely difficult to trust when they have been hurt, abandoned, betrayed and forgotten by their very own fathers and mothers.

As I told Brennan, anger is a destructive coping mechanism that is filling the hearts and minds of his generation.

"Brennan," I said, "I have a friend that used to be a trainer for the San Francisco 49ers. He told me once that before he even begins to train an athlete he first asks, 'Who do you need to forgive?' to which they invariably reply, 'What does forgiveness have to do with physical training?'" My friend then explains that a lack of forgiveness is like poison in the body. It hurts, inhibits, destroys and kills those who are trying to be strong mentally, physically and spiritually. Choosing not to forgive is choosing to poison yourself and if you want to perform at levels of excellence in your life, you must rid yourself of this toxin.

My friend also told the athletes that forgiveness is for their own benefit. It doesn't mean that you accept or condone the actions of the person who hurt you, but rather you choose to release the poison in your body. Again, forgiveness is not primarily for the person who victimizes but it is for the one who has been victimized. Forgiveness is like medicine to an illness—it's purpose is to bring healing.

Brennan and I continued to talk and he honestly wrestled with the thought of forgiving his father. He knew it would be a journey, but he was at least considering taking this radical step.

I shared another story with Brennan about the day I experienced profound insight into the healing nature of forgiveness while watching the Oprah Winfrey show. Oprah shared with her television audience about being emotionally and physically violated between the ages of twelve and fourteen by a trusted uncle.

Oprah spoke with such emotion that I found myself riveted to the television set as her story unfolded. She spoke of how she carried the secret, and the resulting anger and pain of molestation, through much of her adult life until finally coming to the place where she was ready to rid her soul of the anguish her uncle had inflicted on her.

And so, one evening at a family gathering, she performed a symbolic act that brought healing to her life—an action that not only helped her forgive but one that produced great peace in her heart. Without her uncle knowing, she reached out her hand and opened it in his direction, grabbed hold of what he took from her, closed her hand into a fist, and pulled it back toward her chest. This one gesture brought forgiveness and comfort to her heart and mind.

As I told Brennan the story, I reiterated that forgiveness was for him—for his generation of young people.

"You may not be able to turn the clock back on what has happened," I said, "but you *can* choose to forgive what someone has done."

At the close of our meeting, Brennan stretched out his arms to hug me and I reached out to hug him back.

"I love you, Brennan, and I'm proud of you for taking the time to listen," I said.

"I love you too, Mr. Braden. Thank you!"

I've heard many teachers say, "These kids today are disrespectful and I'm not going to put up with it!" I submit to you that the "disrespect" is merely displaced aggression and unforgiveness toward so-called authority. "Disrespect" is often an outward manifestation of internal turmoil. The challenge for a teacher is to separate the person from the behavior. By winning our students' hearts, we "win" the right to teach them that negative behavior, actions, and thoughts towards those in authority will only bring negative consequences.

I believe that there is a longing in the heart of every young person for those in authority over them to feel their pain and frustration. There is indeed a delicate balance between looking past the disrespect and addressing the behavior behind it. But if we do this, we win the privilege of becoming advocates for our students. We will experience the joy of partnering with, and showing them how to walk a path that rises above individual circumstances.

Yes, today's teens desire authentic relationships. As educators we must acknowledge that the institution of family has deteriorated, but we must further acknowledge that our job is to be effective despite this breakdown. If we cultivate an atmosphere of love, support and acceptance in the classroom, we will be modeling positive "family" relationships for our students. Every civilization possesses an intrinsic need for family. When we nurture a "family" milieu, we speak the language of hope to an entire generation.

A chapter on our teen culture today wouldn't be complete without some current and relevant statistics, all of which, can easily be found vis-à-vis a quick search on the Internet:

- Studies have shown that 1 in 8 adolescents struggle with depression.

- Suicide is statistically the 3rd biggest cause of death for teens.

- Teens spend an average of 17 hours a week on the Internet.

- The hours per day that television is on in an average US home: 7 hours, 12 minutes.

- Average amount of time teens spend watching television a day is approximately three hours.

- The number of minutes per week that parents spend in meaningful conversation with their children: 38.5 (American Family Research Council).

- 40% of children are born out of wedlock.

- 90% of 8-16 year-olds have seen porn online—most while doing homework (Pornography Statistics 2003; Family Safe Media).

- 80% of 15-17-year-olds have had multiple hard-core porn exposures (Pornography Statistics 2003; Family Safe Media).

- Illicit teen drug use as of 2003:
    * 8th grade—30.3%
    * 10th grade—44.9%
    * 12th grade—52.8%

- Underage drinking costs the United States more than $58 billion dollars annually; enough for a new state of the art computer for every student.

- In the last thirty days, 50% of teenagers report drinking with 32% being drunk on at least one occasion.

- The Centers for Disease Control (CDC) report that by the age of 20, nearly 75% of teenagers have had sexual intercourse.

- Among seniors in high school, 60.5% of teens have had sexual intercourse (CDC).

- MTV is watched by 73% of boys and 78% of girls ages 12 to 19 and airs (on average) 9 sexual scenes per hour and more than 8 uncensored profanities per hour (Parents Television Council, 2004).

- 40% of American children will go to sleep in fatherless homes (Dr. John Diggs, M.C. 2001).

- 75% of teen boys and 60% of teen girls say they have hit someone within the last 12 months because they were angry.

- 39% of middle school students say they don't feel safe at school.

- On the "No Dad At Home" ABC 20/20 program, with Charles Gibson, it was stated that there are more boys living in America without their fathers than in any other country in the world.

These statistics, while revealing deep rooted and enormously complex issues challenging our young people today, are just the tip of the iceberg. An iceberg is a massive floating body of ice that has broken away from a glacier with only about ten percent of its mass above the surface. What a metaphor! I believe that informed, passionate educators will discern that there is a culture war destroying our young people, but I see valiant teachers placing themselves on the frontlines of this battle each day in an attempt to intervene on behalf of their students.

ᵈBrian Graden, president of MTV programming once said, "I can't help but be worried that we are throwing so much at young adults so fast. There is no amount of preparation or education or even love that you could give a child to be ready."

Despite the glamorization of drug and alcohol use, sexual promiscuity and violent behavior—educators who win the hearts of their students also win the opportunity to empower these young people to make wise choices even in the midst of cultural chaos.

A Gallup Youth Survey in 2004 asked teens where they find motivation: Does it come from within or do you need someone to motivate you? Sixty-seven percent said they find it within while thirty-two percent said they needed someone else to motivate them.

I pose the question: Are we helping to motivate students, or have we relinquished them to a culture of chaos? Some educators argue that the generation has been abandoned. Some argue that the generation has been entitled, and some argue that it's a little of both. Whatever your opinion might be, we can all agree that relinquishing students to the current chaotic culture is unacceptable, irreverent and irresponsible for those of us seeking to make a difference in a child's life.

5

"All About Woo"

TEACHER IN THE MIRROR

"There are more psychologists, psychiatrists and mental health counselors in America today than ever before, yet our culture continues to struggle with issues of violence, dysfunction, poor choices and lack of motivation. Not to take away from the necessity of clinicians, but love transcends understanding. Love is personal. Young people don't just want sympathy, they want to be loved unconditionally—and love is action, not an emotion or pseudo expression. When educators woo—it means that they are seeking to draw their students to them and thereby, as educators, act in accordance with genuine love."

The human heart weighs just less than one pound. It is so small, but so powerful. I once heard a speaker communicate the following random facts about the heart:

- Your heart will beat over 37 million times this year alone.
- Your heart will beat 2.5 billion times by the age of 70.
- Your heart will pump 650,000 gallons of blood this year;

equal to 81 tanker trucks.

- Your heart will generate enough power in 50 years to lift a battle ship out of the water.
- Your heart is discharging more fluid in the next minute than a faucet at full blast.

The heart is a powerful muscle, indeed! A heart feels, a heart senses. It knows gratitude, joy, anger, frustration, depression, passion, hope, peace and love. A coach says, "Your heart isn't in this!" Or a coach says in the fourth quarter, "It's all about heart now!" Someone says, "Don't you have a heart?" Another one says, "You're heartless" and a significant other says, "I love you with all my heart."

In English, there is only one word for love. We say I love you to our spouses but we also say I love McDonald's cheeseburgers. The same four-letter word (love) is used to express relational intimacy just as it is used to express a craving for a particular food. In the Greek language, however, there are multiple words used to express the English word "love." The Greeks term for pure love, with no strings attached is "agape." Agape love is defined as pure and absolute. Agape love is liberating. This truest form of love says, I love you despite...I love you always...I love you even though...

The word the Greeks used for conditional love was called "eros." It is a conditional love that says I love you when...I love you if... It is a "love" that has hooks (conditions) in it, i.e. you give me something and I'll give you something.

Think about your favorite teacher. He/she was not necessarily your favorite teacher because of the content of their lessons, but most likely because of the love they exemplified. You knew they cared about you. This is equally true for the students in our classes. They don't care about how much we know, but how much we care.

Love is sacrificial, but the status quo within our institutions and businesses today is expediency and convenience, not necessarily sacrifice. Sadly, because most of our students have not seen this type of sacrifice, their hearts have a difficult time loving.

How many times have you heard people say in one way or another—it's all about you! Songs, books and CDs all shout this message. Fast food marketing campaigns likewise allude to this (i.e. Burger King's famous, "Have it your way!"). Students today are experiencing "eros" love but they have little or no knowledge of "agape" love.

I contend that it is not "all about you." To believe this is tragically misleading. Instead, I propose that we say, it's *"all about woo."* The former emphasizes self and getting, whereas *"all about woo"* focuses on others and giving in a manner consistent with agape love. I've often challenged teachers to woo students to them. To woo is to "agape" in such a way as to draw students to oneself.

"But how do I love that child? He's unlovable and incapable of being loved." Many educators have said or thought this on more than one occasion.

First of all, never take anything a student does or says personally. Ninety-nine percent of the time, a student's comments and actions are displaced aggression and are the manifestation of internal turmoil stemming from negative cultural and environmental baggage.

I've also heard teachers ask, "But how can I connect with a student when I don't even understand their culture?" This is a fair question but cannot become a deterrent for connecting with a child.

It is true that there are advantages to being culturally competent but it is not necessary in order to woo a child. The most important ingredient in wooing a child is your willingness to love. Anyone who loves can build relationships, no matter the background.

So how do effective teachers woo their students? Listed below are various characteristics and attributes of teachers who have effectively accomplished this task. They are not in any particular order and this is not an exhaustive list by any means. My observations have shown that those teachers who employ most, if not all of these techniques, become life changers for their students. I affectionately call these types of teachers "all aces" or "home-run hitters."

Make Connections

In a day and age when people strive to connect with as many "friends" as possible via social networking sites such as MySpace, Facebook, Twitter, etc., it's rare to see people actually connecting with one another. I'm talking about the type of connection that transcends technological or superficial means. I'm referring to the connection that people have with one another at the deepest level—a level of intimacy. Good teachers seek out and act upon opportunities to connect.

When a connection is made, a strong bond starts to form. Ultimately, the connection evolves into a friendship and fruits of that friendship are loyalty, understanding, and forgiveness, just to name a few. Teachers should develop rich friendships with their students. Not the type of friendship that violates professional standards and conduct, but a familial friendship that fuels kindred spirits and help establish an individual sense of being cared for.

My friend Bob Burke has been teaching for 36 years. He's a master at connecting with kids. I've seen him walk over to a student who was talking to me, politely interrupt, extend his hand and say, "Hi, I'm Mr. Burke. How are you doing?" and then proceed to tell the student where his room is located and that he is available should the student need any help. The ease at which he connects with young people never ceases to amaze me. His boldness and genuine compassion have gained him respect and made him one of the best-loved teachers on campus.

Connections develop when we engage students in conversations about life and learning. They are formed as we become a resource that links students to each other; when we extend ourselves; when we affirm and/or inquire; when we observe changes in students' lives and facilitate personal communication; when we seek to build social networks and emotional stabilities in their lives; and most importantly, connections are made when we show that we are supportive and caring.

All the studies that I have read show that experience or the educational accomplishments of a teacher has nothing to do with students feeling connected. Spending years in the teaching profession and even earning various postgraduate degrees, doesn't mean that an educator will be esteemed by his or her students. I have heard teachers attempt to gain respect from students by trumpeting their own educational accomplishments. While this might impress colleagues, it means nothing to young people! The teacher who does connect meaningfully with their students is the one who woos hearts and minds by infusing a sense of belonging and purpose.

Fair, Reasonable, Respectful

Nothing exasperates a child more than an unfair, unreasonable and disrespectful teacher. Many times when we as teachers are upset with a child, we won't take a reflective step backwards and say, "Am I being objective in this situation?" Rather, we are punitive and often react negatively which the student rightly perceives to be unfair, unreasonable and disrespectful.

Logical consequences for misbehavior, rather than punitive ones, will woo the heart of a child as they recognize that they are being dealt with in a manner that is fair, reasonable and respectful. Nothing diminishes a teacher's credibility faster than disrespect.

I've heard teachers tell students, "I'm the one in authority here!" They use their position of power, whether it's logical or not, to trump a student's will. We, as authority figures, never want to be illogical or make unreasonable statements when attempting to correct a child. Each time a need for correction presents itself, so does the chance for growth and development. A conflict or crisis situation is always an opportunity to woo the heart of a child. If you think about it, true character growth comes not on the mountaintop of life's successes but in the valley of life's troubles.

Teachers should seek to have students own their misbehavior.

To do this, we must never use our position of authority to provoke a child into performing, which, at its core, is nothing more than manipulation. Just as a teacher would never accept behavioral infractions being justified on the part of "youthfulness," so we must never justify our position of authority as the tool to manipulate a child into performing. Our goal is to teach, model and train to do the right thing because it is the right thing—not because one has been manipulated. Doing the right thing is always fair, reasonable and respectful for young and old alike.

I like to think that a teacher always has a "license" to operate with students. It's very similar to a driver's license. As long as we obey the rules of the road we're just fine, but as soon as we violate the rules we're subject to a fine or revocation. The license to operate with students is called respect. The old adage, "If we respect them, then they will respect us," is true. Conversely, it's true as well, that it is very easy for our "license" to be "revoked" by students. Teachers can dismantle in one day everything they've attempted to build in one semester.

We have all witnessed and perhaps even experienced a teacher losing respect because of something they did or said. When this happens, the greatest action a teacher can take to restore respect and trust is to apologize.

I always started each school year by reviewing my classroom policies and procedures with the students. During that time I would tell them that if a situation ever arose wherein I disrespected them in front of their classmates I would publicly apologize to them— even if it meant getting down on one knee and asking them to forgive me. Students are shocked, even bewildered when they hear this for the first time. I would also tell them that one of the greatest signs of strength in any human being is the ability to humbly apologize. And, in my case, an apology is more than just words; it's also an action. Thus, getting down on a knee and looking into the eyes of the offended is a strong symbolic gesture.

There have been several times in my teaching career where I did, in fact, publicly apologize to a student. On a couple of occasions, the apology included getting down on my knee in front of the entire class and asking the offended student to forgive me. Thankfully, they did. But if they hadn't forgiven me, I would have communicated to them and the class that I understood their decision to not forgive. I would have expressed that I knew the decision to forgive was theirs and theirs alone, but that I want them to know that I would spend my time proving to them and the class that I deserved to be forgiven because I was truly remorseful. Students need to see this side of our humanity.

Why would a teacher do something like that? Why would we open ourselves up to student ridicule and/or scrutiny? It's because we want to restore the student/teacher respect that gives us a platform to help individual students come alive. ᵉHoward Thurman said it best when he stated, "What the world needs is people who have come alive." Teachers who respect their students will help them come alive.

Kindness Isn't Weakness

Exemplifying kindness is not a sign of weakness to students—unless you allow it to be. I've heard teachers say that if they're kind to their students, their students will take advantage of them. Allowing students to violate personal boundaries and take advantage of you is weakness—not kindness.

Genuine kindness doesn't come from being timid, lacking core values or operating in fear. Rather, genuine kindness is a manifestation of internal strength. It is an empowering message from one heart to another. Ultimately, it is a strong act of love. Kindness is defined as the act, or the state of being, as marked by charitable behavior and concern for others. To me, kindness is the expression of concern.

Educators who fear that their kindness will be seen as weakness need to clearly communicate to their students that kindness is not a matter of the teacher giving and the students taking, but it is an honorable act that empowers individuals to own their actions without blame and displaced aggression. Kind teachers will always deal with less aggression because kindness deflects anger.

Appropriating kindness also has nothing to do with your particular personality type. I've seen stoic personalities, direct personalities, crass personalities, easy going personalities, charismatic personalities, touchy-feely personalities, etc. all operate in incredible kindness. Although kindness is an action that transcends personality types, it is an act of love that is filtered through the individual's personality. Authentic kindness will always be extended out of principle, not obligation.

I am convinced that kindness will create an atmosphere where students feel the freedom to change. It was kindness shown to me by others that allowed me to change in areas of my life—both personally and professionally. It has changed who I am at the very core. It altered what I do, who I want to become, what I value, how I operate...and the list goes on.

Most educators would agree that classrooms, by their very nature, tend to be anxiety-inducing environments. The personal and professional pressures in a classroom are intense. All teachers have lost their cool at some point in time because students had gotten the best of them. It's easy to allow yourself to get mad and treat students the way they treat you. Real "control" is not caving in to this temptation, but choosing instead to operate in kindness. I challenge you to develop an exemplary kindness about you and your being.

Be Authentic, Be Real, Be Transparent

My friend and long-time teacher, Mr. Marlin Roehl, once told me that personal openness is a bridge for students. I like the metaphor. When teachers are authentic and real we provide a bridge for students to connect with us. Openness always invites! Clarity and candidness are powerful tools that foster relational certainty for students.

When I was a teacher, I would often share my fears and failures with the students. It was always interesting to observe their reactions when I revealed my humanity. Many times I could literally see the sense of freedom and empowerment reflected on their faces as I shared such thoughts. It was like they were thinking, "I've experienced the same fears and failures." It is this type of transparency that allows students to let down their defenses in order to confront their personal struggles with objectivity and courage.

I'll never forget what a tenth grade student said to me after I shared in his class about my fear of not being respected by friends and family.

"But, Mr. Braden," he exclaimed, "How can you be afraid of being disrespected? You can bench press 500 pounds and squat 1000!"

The entire class and I just laughed. He got the point that I had made and now he was seizing an opportunity to woo my heart to his using humor. And woo it he did. A bridge had been built—a bridge that I started and he completed. It can be said that there is no greater joy for a teacher than when our students reciprocate the love and affection that we have for them.

Ask and Listen

I remember a few years back talking to a student in the front office of the junior high school where I taught. Yvette was her name and she was waiting to speak to the principal. As I stopped by to pick up my mail, I engaged her in conversation.

"Yvette!" I began, and then proceeded with two minutes worth of popcorn questions—one question after another in rapid fire. I learned this active listening technique from my mother who is a great conversationalist.

"Yvette, how's your day going?" When she didn't respond,

I continued, "You look tired—what time did you go to bed last night?"

--She answered.

"You look awesome for only having five hours of sleep last night."

--She laughed.

"What do you do late at night?"

--She communicated that she usually talked to her friends.

And so the questions went—one right after the other. I started to walk out of the office when I heard the secretary say to me, "Unbelievable!"

I stopped and turned toward the secretary who had been listening to the conversation. Smiling, I asked, "Did you learn anything about the life a junior high student today?

"I don't know how you do it, Mr. Braden," she said.

"I learned it from my mother. You can blame her for nurturing it in my life." We both laughed.

Questions, in general, open a student's world. When you ask your students questions, you reveal that you are interested in them as individuals. Don't assume that too many inquiries might be construed as prying. If they ask you why you're asking all the questions, then tell them the truth—you want to know more about them because they are valuable and have a story to tell.

Your students are always free to respond however they would like. Because they are free moral agents, they can ignore you, reveal the truth, or lie to you. But even if they are giving you the "go away" behavioral signal, continue to express a keen interest in their lives. Most of the time, people like to talk about themselves.

The questions I asked Yvette formed a connection with her. She saw and heard my responses to her answers, and she valued the interest I had in her life. Yvette experienced validation and affirmation from me. She walked away from the conversation knowing that a teacher truly cared about her...and I truly did.

Read Their Mail

"Reading their mail" is, of course, a figurative expression. It is a way of letting them know that you understand what they are thinking and feeling and you are concerned.

My wife loves it when I'm able to communicate to her what she's feeling. In a sense, students feel the same way. As students develop their own personhood, it is often a struggle for them to give voice to their particular feelings and dilemmas. A teacher who can "read a student's mail" and help them articulate what they're experiencing will make a connection with the student.

Several years ago I was privileged to have Miguel as a student. He was disconnected, so much so, that when he would show up to class all he would do is sit at his desk and observe his surroundings. Miguel rarely spoke and never turned in an assignment, much less take notes in class. I never received a single piece of paper with his name on it nor did I observe Miguel doing anything else that had to do with academic performance. Ironically, he was never disruptive—he just wouldn't engage.

If you asked Miguel to share with his classroom partner he would reply, "I'm all right." If you asked him to take notes, he would say, "That's OK, Mr. Braden." As I grew to understand Miguel I learned that his resistance to doing assigned tasks in class wasn't directed toward me per se. He was just disconnected with life. Miguel was a likable, handsome young man who had friends, but his family life was so negative that it impacted every other adult relationship that he had.

One day, Miguel didn't show up for class so after school, I drove to his home to check on him. When I arrived, I found him in the backyard. He was sitting on a chair next to an adult male who had a beer in his hand. I asked Miguel why he wasn't at school; he got up out of his chair, and motioned for me to talk with him in the front yard.

"Mr. Braden," he said, "My mother just left her boyfriend (pointing to the adult male in the backyard) and she hooked up with this other guy from Arizona. She just moved there to live with her new boyfriend but she wants me to live with him (again pointing to the adult male in the backyard). It's ok though because I'd rather be here with him than with my mom."

I couldn't believe what I was hearing.

Miguel's father had been incarcerated for most of Miguel's life; thus, he was out of the picture and still had seven more years to serve before being released from prison. Basically, Miguel was raising himself. After chatting for about ten minutes, I asked Miguel to walk with me to the front yard and I proceeded to "read his mail."

"Miguel," I said, "You're father and mother have failed you. I'm not judging anybody, but you've been abandoned. This isn't normal. In fact, you're entire life has been spent trying to create stability for yourself and your sister. You've lived in fear of the unknown your whole life. How can you trust others when you can't even trust your own father and mother? You fear your mom's next destructive act, you fear that you'll never be successful in life and you're tired of believing in empty promises. I know you feel dead on the inside. I'm only saying this to say, Miguel, I may not be your father but I love you as a father would a son and I will do everything I can in my power to make you believe that your life will one day be free from these unnecessary fears and all this instability. You may feel that nobody cares, but that's not true. I care about you."

A tear ran down Miguel's cheek and he was responsive to my words. After our talk, I bought him a sandwich from a nearby hamburger joint and headed home for the night. He promised me that he would be at school the next day, and sure enough, he was.

The next day at school, a teacher friend and I put together some gifts, wrapped them in paper and presented them to Miguel. One gift was a three ring binder, another some paper, one gift had pencils and pens and another was an "easy" button from Staples. You know—the big red button that once is pushed says, "That was easy!" Miguel loved the easy button. He got a kick out of it. By semester's end, Miguel had only missed two days of school in both our classes. He ended up getting a B in my class, which he worked very hard for. I won this young man's heart by "reading his mail."

By the way, I'm proud to say that Miguel graduated from high school and today owns his own lucrative tree cutting business.

In my days as a history teacher, I always found it rewarding to make life applications for my students from the California State

History standards. It afforded me a platform to express my awareness of the struggles and challenges young people face.

Throughout the years, I have consistently told my students that History is narrative. It is the human experience—the collective stories of groups and of individual people. History is two words combined—his and story. There are always life lessons to be learned from history.

So, for example, when teaching a unit about the Industrial Revolution and the injustices of unfair labor practices for blue-collar workers and young children, I made life application to similar wrongdoings and struggles in the lives of my students. I noticed that when I spoke about my students' personal struggles, I saw their mental and emotional wheels turning and I knew that I was helping them make sense of their frustration. I was, in effect, "reading their mail." They were probably thinking, "How does he know what's going on in my mind or how does he know what I'm feeling?" Seizing opportunities to communicate in this manner is part of "reading their mail."

Crisis situations are also opportune times for teachers to "read their students' mail." It may take a few questions and some probing, but sooner or later you will get enough information to help your student make sense of their pain and/or frustration. Most of the time the student will walk away saying to themselves, "My teacher understands me." And that is what we want our students to recognize. You and I both know that the reason we understand is because we, like our students, live lives filled with experiences—good and bad, and these experiences shape and give us understanding. "Wooing" takes place when students feel that we understand them.

Another crucial part of "reading their mail" is discernment. We must be aware of the verbal and non-verbal clues that our students present so that we are able to assist them in identifying the best course of action for their situation or dilemma.

Body Language

What kind of body language are you displaying to your kids? When I first started teaching, my master teacher told me, "Never let them see you smile until Thanksgiving," and he wasn't joking! WC Fields is reported to have said, "Start every day with a smile and get it over with." Maybe I should have suggested this little bit of advice to my master teacher.

Both of these statements might make you laugh...and that's a good thing because smiles are the doorway to affirmation. I once heard a teacher say, "The shortest distance between two people is a smile." Smiles attract but frowns, scowls and grimaces push people away. Smiling changes moods, it is contagious and it relieves stress.

Many of our students never experience a genuine smile of affection from their family members. Often it is the teachers who are left to influence a child's self-system positively with smiles, hugs and affirming body language.

Emotional Hot Buttons

So much of life for young people is the affective domain—the self-system, the emotional. I have found that students all have an emotional hot button, and once you hit it, they process thoughts of acceptance or rejection.

Prior to communicating a directive to a student, I will strive to hit their emotional hot button. It can be with a brief verbal affirmation like, "I think the world of you." Or, "You are incredibly bright. You have the ability to take something that is so difficult to understand and break it down." It can also be something as informal as, "I love your shoes," or, "That's such a cute bracelet." The comment doesn't even have to flow. It just has to hit the "right" emotional hot button.

Emotional hot buttons are very different for each child and it's important to watch the body language of a child to know if you're hitting your mark or hitting a raw nerve. If you feel that you have hit a raw nerve, quickly clarify and bring the attention back to yourself.

For example, several years ago one of my students received a significant new hairstyle over the weekend. Instead of her hair going down to the middle of her back she now had a layered, shoulder length cut. I made a positive comment to her regarding the style. She was with her friends and looked at me sheepishly—as if she didn't want me to say anything else and draw more attention to her. I knew I had hit the wrong emotional button. So I quickly took the attention off of her and made fun of myself. I said, "At least you've got hair to cut. I'm bald." All the girls laughed and she smiled. I later apologized to her in private. She opened up about how she had been teased by people all day because of her haircut. I was happy that I had been given an opportunity to encourage her. Even though I failed to hit the right emotional hot button initially, I still had a later opportunity to win her heart by listening and empathizing with her frustrations.

Mysterious But Consistent

It sounds contradictory, doesn't it? Be mysterious and yet, consistent. Let me explain this through some random thoughts I have regarding this concept.

- Allow room for discovery over a period of time instead of all at once.

- Don't let your students define you. They hate being defined so don't allow yourself to be defined.

- Be subject to change. Let them experience your creativity by being open to change.

- Be consistent with your rules but spontaneous with fun. Be crazy and consistent; be funny and serious.

- Show all sides to your humanity and don't play the role of a boring and conservative educator. It is too distant.

- Don't play the role of judge or president. It is too legalistic. Embrace the role of a success coach; a life coach. You are in the trenches together. You are competing together. You are growing together.

- Empower positive interdependence with them.

- Don't create distance. There is already too much distance in the world. Our labels create emotional distance.

- Be one of them. Let them say about you, "He/she understands me. He/she is on my side. He/she is a mentor to me."

Use Humor

Anything that leads to laughing, smiling or feeling a sense of amusement is humor. Humor is an effective form of communication that has the power to ease tensions and create an environment for engaged learning.

Successful teachers play off their students' comments, tell personal anecdotes that poke fun at themselves and do outrageous things. They are playful and lighthearted, focused on fostering an informal classroom, a give and take classroom, and are not afraid to tell a joke or two.

When teachers use humor to set the classroom stage, students are able to relax and tend to listen and learn better. It is important to be yourself. The best humor comes from your own personality and your own experiences.

Project Hope

You and I project our presence every day in the way that we sit, talk, walk and stand. Projecting an attitude of hope will woo your students. For many kids, the only projection of hope in their daily lives comes from a teacher who expresses it via an attitude, perspective or worldview. Teachers have a tremendous responsibility to cast and create a vision of hope. It might be as easy as communicating one sentence, or as difficult as walking alongside a stubbornly defiant child who needs to be held accountable day in and day out.

We know that one cannot truly live without hope. Hope is a vital and fundamental necessity for every child—in every place on the earth. I read an article many years ago about the travesty of Romanian orphanages. The article told about infants lying in cribs all day.

As a result, these neglected babies were emotionless and lifeless even when faced with incidents that would bring tears to a nurtured child. I found it to be quite moving, for in so many ways, this is a picture of many of our students. The need for projecting hope is often overwhelming.

A superintendent for a former district in which I was employed had a mission for each teacher, administrator and staff member. The mission statement became a cliché but she would say, "All the students all the time." I loved the catchy phrase because it reminded me that I needed to build up my students all the time. I put the quote on a small post-it note in the upper right hand corner of my lectern and read it everyday. Now I know that there is a plethora of ways to interpret the quote, but I chose to see it as a motivational encouragement in projecting hope in the lives of my students. My thinking was that hope was always in the best interests of my students and it would always edify.

To this day, I can't think of a better way to build kids than to give them hope and the resulting promise of a bright future. Hope is an encourager. It is fundamental for life change. For many youngsters, their present situation is bleak and they cannot begin to imagine the existence of a positive, hope-filled future.

A teacher painting a portrait of hope to kids might sound like the following: "I see greatness in you." "You have a future and a hope." "Greatness is around the corner for you." "You're going to be a great leader." "You're going to make a great dad/mother." "A company would be lucky to have someone with your talents." "Your ability to get along is going to bring you great friendships and relationships throughout your life." "You're a hard worker and this is going to make you successful one day." "You're a great listener and that's what people love." "You make the tough decisions and people will seek this in leaders." "You're not out to hurt people but you stand up for what you believe. This trait will make your life rich." "At the rate you're going, you'll not only have your Bachelor's degree but you'll have a Master's degree as well." "You have the ability to be in management one day, if that's what you would like." "With your creativity and work ethic, I see you having the home of your dreams."

And the list goes on. The bottom line is that a foundation of hope has been laid and vision has been cast. Day in and day out, we must continue to keep this vision of hope in the forefront of our students' minds.

Change Their Perceptions

Over the years, I have worked with many students that have been affiliated with or involved in violent gangs. Gangsters walk into any particular room and visually scan it, radar fashion. They also use posture and pose as a means to impress, intimidate and/or victimize. These students have never been empowered with the life-skills to cohabitate in a caring and reciprocating environment. Their perception of life is "survival of the fittest." It's a "dog eat dog" world philosophy and a predatory type mindset. They have been hurt and operate under the perception that they need to hurt back. Essentially, they prove the well-known concept that hurt people will *hurt* people. Although it is very difficult to change a student's perception, it is necessary if they are to grow into loving and civil minded adults.

I am not surprised at the violence that we see in our culture today because of these negative perceptions. They don't form overnight; rather, they are established over months and years. Additionally, the groundwork was laid long before a major act of violence springs forth. There are many factors involving physiological, economic and social conditions that contribute to these false but complex perceptions.

If we all agree that perception changes attitude and attitude affects behavior, then we must attack negative perceptions. To do this, we can begin by helping kids recognize why certain perceptions are wrong and why certain perceptions are hurtful.

I've told students, on many occasions, that if they have been hurt, victimized or abused, then they will most likely do the same to those who surround them because that is what the sociological studies reveal. I tell them, "You blame your parents for hurting you and yet you're going to grow up and do the same thing to your children!" I also explain to them that the path to breaking this destructive cycle is to literally change the way they think because thoughts affect emotions and ultimately, will control behaviors.

I'm reminded that kids are kids. They all like ice cream, movies and pop corn, but the same kid who asks you how you're doing at school in the morning, can be the kid that kills over gang colors after school in the afternoon. It is a paradox to so many of us and yet, it is reality—and it all has to do with perception. Sometimes we get too clinical when dealing with young people and the "all business" approach is often irrelevant to them.

The personal approach takes time, but is one of the most effective ways to change perceptions. We've all heard the definition of insanity: Doing the same thing over and over but expecting different results. Do we expect to change teens' negative perceptions by continuing to do the same-old, same-old? It's important for us to look for new methods to change students' perceptions. Thinking outside of the box and coloring outside of the lines should be our mantra when it comes to exploring ways to change negative perceptions.

In every war there is an enemy, and sometimes we, as professionals, are our own worst enemies. We allow our students to hold onto faulty perceptions without attempting to transform their thinking. We also inhibit ourselves as educators when we fail to understand why they think what they think.

Let me explain.

I recently sat through a Gang-Awareness training session presented by a local non-profit organization. The facilitator, Mr. Tony Ortiz, told a story about a teen who was afraid to go to school because of the intimidation and threats that he felt from rival gangbangers. The Southern California transplanted teen had been affiliated with *Surenos,* but he and his family moved to a new city and into a *Norteno* neighborhood. Each day, the young man would catch the bus at the local bus stop and be dropped off at school. Then he would catch the bus after school, and return to his original stop.

On two occasions, however, *Norteno* gang members jumped the teen as soon as he got off the bus at school. So without consulting his parents or anyone else, he made the executive decision to stop going to school. Most teens would tell their parents about such intimidation and brutality but this teen didn't feel that he had an advocate in his family, so he kept the information to himself. The young teen was being raised by an alcoholic father who, rather than listen, would shut his son down by telling him to fight, not run. At least, that was the son's perception, so he made the decision to avoid the bus and school altogether. Most of us, given the same circumstances and the same futile parenting would probably have made the same decision.

According to the teen's English teacher, the young man performed fairly well at school and had the capacity to be an excellent student. The teacher/student relationship was good, but the teacher always wondered why the student didn't attend school on a regular basis. One day, Mr. Ortiz, a behavioral interventionist and gang counselor with whom the young man also had a good relationship with, asked the teen if he believed that education was a good thing.

"Yes!" was his answer.

"Isn't school the place you're supposed to go to get educated?"

"Yes," the teen again replied.

"Then why aren't you going to school?"

"Because I've been jumped twice by the *Nortenos*!"

After finding out about the intimidation and violence, Mr. Ortiz had a conversation the following day with the student's English teacher revealing to her the teen's challenges and why he hadn't been at school.

"I think you should give the kid an award certificate for not coming to school," said the good spirited Mr. Ortiz to the English teacher.

The teacher was perplexed by his comment.

"Seriously," Mr. Ortiz continued with a smile on his face, "this kid is making a good decision in not coming to school. He's preserving his life!"

After this conversation, the English teacher came up with an idea that she shared with Mr. Ortiz. It was an "outside the box" idea and he commended her for reaching out to the teen.

"What if I give a packet containing a week's worth of work to him and he can turn it in whenever he feels safe to show up to school? Even if he had to miss school for personal reasons, he could still get credit for the completed work."

This worked for the teen. As the community of gang counselors, teachers and social services reached out to the young man and his family, many false perceptions were radically changed and new ones began to evolve. For several weeks, the student would complete his packets of work, and turn them into his teachers and eventually gang counselors working with the gangbanger perpetrators created a permanent resolution. It took a community of caring educators and counselors willing to change their perceptions and to influence others to change theirs in order for transformation to take place.

In this particular story, it all started with a gang counselor and a teacher who had a passion to understand a kid's perception. As a result, the student experienced a new perception—one of advocacy. Sometimes we become so formalized and clinical, that we're not any good *practically* speaking; and sometimes we become so informal that we're not any good *clinically* speaking. The bottom line is that winning the heart of a child gives us the opportunity to change their destructive perceptions and help them establish new ones that are respectful and responsible.

6

"Never Forget"

TEACHER IN THE MIRROR

    History has recorded and memorialized great rally cries and slogans that evoke emotion, cause, passion, and response; such as, "Remember the Alamo!" or "No taxation without representation!" In an educational sense—what is your rally cry? What drives you and reminds you of the hills you're willing to die on? What memorialized incidences have you experienced in the trenches that have evolved to become your battle cry—your "Never Forgets?"

    I recently had a conversation with my friend, Manny. Manny has been in education for thirty-six years as a teacher, an administrator and a district official. As we sat in my new office, and he was congratulating me on my new principalship and the task at hand, I noticed that he was wearing two watches.

    "Manny," I laughed, "You have two watches on!" You have to know him to know that it was quite possible he had put the two watches on by accident...anything was possible with Manny. Everyone liked my friend. His pleasant personality and gentle disposition made him a target for jokesters—and Manny, who didn't have a mean bone in his body, always took the jokes in stride. My amusement didn't offend Manny, but it did stop him midsentence.

"Manny," I continued, "Why are you wearing two watches?"

Manny paused, looked down for a moment, and then solemnly answered me. I could tell by the sound of his voice and his body posture that the wearing of his two watches was calculated and personal.

"Scott, every day I wear two watches. The one on my left wrist tells me what time it is, while the watch on my right wrist reminds me of how special time is. It helps me to never forget."

Three years earlier, Manny's son had been tragically killed while serving a tour of duty in Iraq. His son was an Army soldier—an honorable and decorated one at that—and the tragedy impacted Manny like nothing ever before. In subsequent months, Manny developed a fresh appreciation for life and a passion for experiencing the uniqueness of each day, and the watches on his wrists were a reminder to never forget.

Like Manny, I have my "never forget watches," only they aren't watches...rather, they are students. My "never forgets" are etched in my mind and they remind me why I do what I do and why I must keep doing it. For me, there are two students whose lives continually motivate me to reach the numerous young people who are disconnected, disenfranchised, disheartened and depressed. The names of my two "never forget" students are Sarah and Thomas.

First, let me share Sarah's story. Sarah was the embodiment of human intelligence and physical beauty. She had lush, beautiful brown hair and big brown puppy dog eyes. She was absolutely stunning but she was also bright, articulate and funny. Although Sarah was gorgeous on the outside, on the inside she felt as though she was a throwaway.

Sarah was fifteen years old, and I was in my second year of teaching when she became my student. Childless at that point, my wife and I considered all our students to be our "children," but Sarah was a student that my wife and I would have adopted. She had all the gifts, talents and abilities we wanted our very own children to possess. The only thing missing in Sarah's life, or so we thought, was guidance, nurturing and adults who spoke and acted with honesty and support.

Sadly, Sarah's father was just another random trick for her mother; a prostitute and drug addict who promptly abandoned her at birth. Sarah's grandmother took her in, but was abusive and abrasive, militant and conditional. As a result, throughout her fifteen years of life, Sarah had never known love. As happens so often in young people with Sarah's background, her entire life revolved around acceptance from her peers. As a cheerleader, she was validated for her good looks, but she struggled to find acceptance outside of the shallow and short-lived affirmation of the teenage crowd.

Over time, Sarah began to make compromising choices. In her tenth grade year alone, I saw Sarah make one bad decision after another—decisions like drinking, drugs, and promiscuous behavior.

At the time, my wife and I taught at the same school. Many days Sarah would come to our classrooms and share her typical adolescent challenges, but my heart always went out to her because she never truly felt loved.

I remember one particular occasion when Sarah sat in my classroom and told me about the prior night and how she had done something that she believed was really bad. She never told me what it was exactly, but she did communicate that she felt like a throwaway.

I looked at Sarah, paused, and said, "Sarah, we have all done things that we're not proud of. I have skeletons in my closet—but they don't define who I am today." I continued, "You know you're special—you believe that don't you?"

She looked hesitantly at me before replying, "Mr. Braden...I don't feel special."

Nothing is more important than a sense of belonging and a sense of importance to a young person, a true sense of feeling special. Sarah had none of these. She thought of herself as something of an object, even expendable, and although she felt repulsed by the thought of being used and tossed aside, she routinely caved in to the cultural temptations that were destroying her. No amount of positive intervention or truthful perspective from a teacher seemed to change the way she perceived herself. Sarah was truly a throwaway in her own mind, and because of this self-identity, no amount of help seemed to alter the destructive behavior she was choosing.

Within two weeks of our talk, Sarah was expelled from school. I didn't see Sarah for several months until one day in June. School was out and my wife and I were shopping at a mall in San Mateo, California. As we were leaving one store and beginning to enter another, I saw Sarah.

She looked different—very different. It didn't take much discernment to realize that something had changed drastically in Sarah's life. Scantily dressed, excessive and overdone makeup, it was as if she had purposely tried to eradicate every semblance of innocence, and in its place she wore a heavy cloak of guilt and shame.

I leaned towards my wife, pointed, and said with excitement, "Honey, there's Sarah."

She was walking with her friend, Jeanette, but when we made eye contact, Sarah turned abruptly and walked quickly in the opposite direction catching us completely off guard. We could do nothing but watch her disappear into the crowd. Jeanette continued walking toward us and gave us a friendly hug and an enthusiastic greeting.

But Sarah never reappeared. She had left the mall.

As we talked with Jeanette the picture became painfully clear as to why Sarah chose to walk away. Sarah lived wherever she could—sometimes with her twenty-five year-old boyfriend in his grandmother's trailer, sometimes in hotel rooms, or, when things were really bad, on the streets of San Mateo. In short, Sarah had become a drug-addicted prostitute, just like her very own mother.

After our conversation with Jeanette, my wife suggested that we make a serious effort to find Sarah and invite her into our home. My heart was responsive, but in all honesty, I had reservations. I wanted things to be safe, orderly and full of accountability—something a drug-addicted prostitute would openly defy. But, since we both wanted Sarah to be in a safe place we set out to find her and have her live with us.

We drove the streets of San Mateo hour after hour, looking in alleyways and main streets, asking person after person, but we didn't find Sarah that night. Days, weeks and months went by, until one chilling, unforgettable night.

It was the night I was contacted by Matt, a former student of mine and a former classmate of Sarah's.

"Mr. Braden, this is Matt. I have some bad news to share with you. Sarah was murdered!"

"What? What happened?" I was stunned.

Numbness and disbelief flowed like a river of ice through my being as every emotion ran rampant. As Matt shared the facts that he knew, my stomach began to cramp, my blood started to boil and my mind raged with anger. To this day, I can still feel the pain of Matt's devastating words, "Sarah was murdered!"

Please allow me to communicate Sarah's "never forget" story as I do when I speak to teenagers all across the United States and in various countries around the world. To my audience it has become known as "Sarah's story."

"Sarah had run off to Las Vegas, Nevada...certainly no place for a little girl. And that's what Sarah was. She was once somebody's little girl. As I tuck my young children into bed every night I tell them how special they are to me...and they believe it. Sarah was special too—priceless, really. But she refused to believe that truth, choosing, instead, to view herself as an object. Well, in Las Vegas she was an object all right...a little girl in a big man's world; a world filled with twisted desire, manipulation and lies. Sarah's

life was more valuable than being used by men for their evil intents and purposes, but because she believed that she had no value, she became what she thought she was—a throwaway.

You know, if you think you are...you are.

Sarah had a fake identification card that stated she was 25 years of age, and she looked every bit of 25. She was absolutely beautiful. Police had picked her up for soliciting on more than one occasion, even going so far as to literally beg her to return to California and leave behind the lifestyle of drugs and prostitution that was destroying her.

Sarah would typically meet men in bars and invite them to her hotel room. She would always ask for the money up front, put it in her pocket, and then perform the services. On the night she died, a painter from Oakland, California met Sarah in a bar. After a few drinks, he took her to a hotel room and he asked her how much—as if you can put a price tag on a little girl's life. She quoted the price and he gave her the cash. She put it in her pocket and proceeded to perform the services.

That's when things got real dark...out of control dark. He started beating Sarah with his bare hands, one punch at a time. He choked her and tossed her around like she was a piece of worthless meat. This continued until Sarah lay on the floor, her body broken beyond repair. And then, as if stealing her life wasn't enough, this man rifled through her pant pockets and took the money he had given to her, and left that little girl in a crumpled, lifeless heap. She was MY little girl!

Today, the man from Oakland who killed my little girl is serving life in prison. But, that doesn't bring Sarah back. If it were *possible, I know Sarah would walk up to this stage, look at you in the eyes, and communicate what I'm sharing with you today. She would say, 'Do not believe the lies that people have told you. You are special! You are valuable! There is a purpose to your life! And, don't you ever give up!'"*

These are the words that I speak to teens about Sarah. They are graphic but all so true. It is Sarah's tragic life that reminds me that I must always fight to defeat the lies that my students like Sarah, tend to believe. I've often wondered what Sarah's life would have turned out to be if my wife and I had found her on the streets of San Mateo that frustrating night.

Because of Sarah, my conversations with students are now deeper, more real, more vital and filled with a greater sense of urgency. I feel that I honor Sarah's life when I tell her story—even in all its excess and chaos.

Over the years, I've had young ladies confide in me that Sarah's story was the inspiration that kept them going—girls like fifteen year old Nikki in Fort Kent, Maine or seventeen year old Maria in Pittsburgh, Pennsylvania. Each time I hear these testimonies, and others like them, I am reminded of the necessity to keep sharing Sarah's story.

Indulge me, once again, as I share another "never forget" story. My student Thomas had a smile that reached from coast to coast, and a personality bigger than a Texas football stadium. He was a swimmer, a water polo player, in addition to being an excellent student. He was everybody's friend. His wit and humor captivated his peers. His one-liners and idiomatic expressions would set even the most anxious hearts at peace. I learned all this information about Thomas after the fact.

Thomas had a gentle disposition and a remarkable appearance. This genuine and fun-loving teenager dressed fashionably, fished and hunted with his father and shopped with his mother. He loved camping with his family and spending time with his friends. He appeared to be an All-American boy.

In the middle of his junior year, Thomas changed high schools. He had begun to hang around a pretty rough crowd, so his mother thought that it would be best for him to move across town and enroll in the high school that his father had graduated from.

I met Thomas on a spring day, during third period. I was sitting at my desk, working on the computer on this normal, mundane day...and then it changed. Not the typical kind of change with unexpected turns and unknown twists that one can navigate without much thought, but the kind of change that is simply overwhelming and debilitating. One you wouldn't wish on your worst enemy.

My secretary informed me that the choir teacher needed help with two students who were having a verbal altercation in class. I was out of my chair and at the classroom in seconds. When I arrived the teacher had both boys separated in the middle of the doorway and explained that there was a war of words happening between them, which included the use of inappropriate language. Fearing that the verbal altercation could escalate into a full-blown physical confrontation, he had called me. A sure sign that a volatile situation is about to go from bad to worse is when students have their camera phones out...and, sure enough, camera phones were out.

After I removed both boys from the classroom, I turned to Thomas and asked what was going on.

"This kid keeps making rude comments and I'm not going to put up with it anymore," was his reply.

"Rude comments?" The other teen exclaimed, "What are you talking about? You're the one texting my girlfriend all sorts of s&#$!"

At that point I decided to walk both boys back to the administrative office to continue the investigation.

The text message that Thomas sent to the other teen's girlfriend was profane, crude and downright uncivil. Quite honestly, I was sickened when I read the comments. And although Thomas had never met the girl or even seen her before for that matter, he was talking "trash" about her in an effort to demoralize her boyfriend.

When all was said and done, both boys agreed that their disruptive behavior was deserving of a suspension. After we worked through the conflict in my office, the young men shook hands and expressed to me and to each other that it was over.

Or so we thought.

After suspending both boys and having their parents pick them up, the girl's parents were on the phone with me wanting to take this situation all the way to the Superintendent's office. Coincidentally, the young ladies' mother worked for an attorney and was well versed in legal terminology. She expressed that there would be recourse should we fail to act appropriately. After a very lengthy conversation, and after the mother had some time to cool down, I suggested that the parents of both teens come to school to make amends "old school" style. She agreed, so I made the arrangements.

Later that day, Thomas' father and stepmother arrived at the school, as did the young lady and her parents. Interestingly enough, Thomas' father was profusely apologetic. He stated that he hadn't raised his son to be insensitive and he would do everything possible to make amends. He even pulled out a letter that he had Thomas write prior to the meeting. Thomas' demeanor was humble and contrite and he handled the written apology like a champion. His humble words were worthy of forgiveness. The young ladies parents, impressed by the letter, became convinced that Thomas was a great kid with a great family and that he had just made a bad decision.

Our conversation that day was loving, appropriate and professional between both sets of parents and both teens. I can truthfully say that I had never walked away from a meeting more encouraged by the way parents and students handled a situation "old school" style.

I must confess that I figuratively patted myself on the back for bringing a volatile situation to a successful and reconcilable resolution. I went home that night and shared the story with my wife and commented to her how I wished more parents would reconcile differences by doing what I saw happen earlier in the day. And, my wife was in total agreement.

Twenty-four hours after the meeting, I received a phone call from my youth services officer. Officer Collins had an office two doors down from mine at school, but he was out of the office and calling me from his cell phone.

"Braden," he said.

"What's up?" I responded.

"I need you to look on SASI (our data program) and tell me if we have a student by the name of Thomas Smith."

"I know we do. I just suspended him yesterday. Why? What's up?" I asked.

"He just killed himself!"

The silence stretched between us like a frozen rope. I was horrified...in complete and utter disbelief. Like a surfer tossed around by the waves after a major spill, I was literally gasping for air. I felt as though I had been sucker punched and kicked in the belly!

Within twenty-four hours of what I thought was reconciliation between parties at odds, an unimaginable tragedy had occurred.

"What happened?" I asked Officer Collins.

"He shot himself in the head."

"Where are you right now?" I asked.

"I'm heading over to his father's house. It happened about thirty minutes ago. You might want to meet me over there."

A district psychologist followed me over to Thomas' house. Police were swarming in and around the house while Thomas' father and stepmother stood arm-in-arm in the front yard. It was surreal. I parked my truck, got out, and walked toward Thomas' parents. The three of us embraced and wept. All I could say was, "I'm so sorry!"

I knew the possibility existed that Thomas' parents would displace the emotional trauma of the tragedy onto me—the administrator who had disciplined their son, but to my surprise, his father kept saying, "This is nobody's fault. Nobody saw this coming. This was Thomas' decision and he needed help."

I later learned that to shift focus away from the suspension, Thomas' dad had taken him shopping the night before. They ran some errands and had an enjoyable father-son time together. Thomas had gotten up that morning and baked cookies for his father to take to work. As part of his punishment for being suspended, his father asked Thomas to clean all the house windows. They had shared a great breakfast and had even exchanged words of affection before his father left. By one-thirty in the afternoon— Thomas was gone. As they say, a permanent solution to a temporary problem.

At Thomas' request, on the day he was suspended, I had him talk to a gay teenager whom he had mocked in the choir room prior to his confrontation with the other teen. Thomas wanted to apologize to the young man saying that he never truly meant the hurtful comments he had made. Their conversation was positive and there was reconciliation, but ironically, as the young man walked back to class, Thomas took me aside and said, "Mr. Braden, you might want to keep an eye on him. There's a lot going on in his life and I think he might be suicidal."

How those words haunt me today! At the time, I had not one hint, nor was there any discernable evidence that he might have been referring to himself.

As I drove home from Thomas' house, I couldn't help but analyze my actions to see if they had played a role in his tragic decision. I walked into my front door, embraced my wife and hugged my children. I spent the rest of that night talking to my wife, and when we finally went to bed, I cried in her arms.

I couldn't sleep, tortured by all the "what-if's." Finally at 2 a.m., after fighting a losing battle against the urge to go to Thomas' house, I got up, got in my truck and made the drive.

Cruising slowly past his darkened home, I felt the family's pain all over again as I tried to imagine what his father must have been feeling, or how his mother felt the day she gave birth to him—all the hopes and dreams they had for their boy. I had hoped to find peace but ultimately, all I succeeded in doing was compounding the deep sadness I had in my heart for this senseless loss of life.

Thomas is another "never forget."

Each and every one of us who has spent much time in education, has had a Thomas or a Sarah who has profoundly impacted their lives. They remind us of the volatility surrounding each fragile and impressionable child. I have challenged myself to be on alert, to be discerning and to surround my students with great people and resources. I tell myself each day that I must reach those students who are being swallowed by darkness and gasping to breathe, barely hanging onto life. I tell myself every day, that a day at school is so much more than a formative assessment, a benchmark or a unit of study—it's about winning hearts and minds. I must treat every conversation I have with a student as if it is my last opportunity to converse with that particular child. In every conversation, I want them to feel loved and to believe that there is purpose to their lives.

I have two "never forgets." I will do whatever it takes to keep from having a third.

7

"Find Your Own Calcutta"

TEACHER IN THE MIRROR

The key to living a rewarding life is finding your purpose. Purpose guides, directs and motivates. Purpose is finding the intersection between your strengths, passion and causes. Is your purpose driving your life or is life driving your purpose?

The train ride from New Delhi, India to Calcutta was long—real long. As the train rattled along the tracks, my bones felt like they were being crushed. My head felt like it had swollen to the size of a beach ball and my joints pulsated with paralyzing pain, exacerbated by a particularly virulent respiratory infection. Complicating matters further was the fact that the trip was over sixteen hours long. The high fever, the aching, the coughing, the sleeplessness and everything else I was experiencing made this journey highly uncomfortable, but I thought to myself, "This is what I love to do; I love cultural experiences and more joyous than anything is the opportunity to lead and facilitate learning experiences for others."

SCOTT BRADEN

In 2001, I organized and conducted this trip that made it possible for thirty-five California students to experience the great country of India. One of my goals for the trip was to visit Mother Teresa's Home for the Destitute and Dying, so that my students would have an opportunity to serve in a third world country. I wanted them to find value in giving and serving rather than taking and being served, which is so common in the American culture. It was September of the year 2000 when I first arranged for the trip and by late July of 2001 thirty-five students were experiencing the culture shock of a lifetime. But, they were finding themselves.

Calcutta was the place Mother Teresa called home. She left her native country when she was nineteen years old with the intention of giving herself to the poor of India. And give she did. Her service and sacrifice was unprecedented, and forever humanity will honor and respect Mother Teresa's selflessness and service to those who were poor, abandoned, rejected and sick. It was Mother Teresa who said that she saw Jesus in every living being. Mother Teresa started a home and hospital for those who were impoverished and in the final stages of dying.

On the train ride to Calcutta, I sat next to a wealthy Indian businessman and engaged in friendly and meaningful conversation. He was amused at my undertaking with thirty-five American students and I was intrigued with his knowledge of cultural facts and the impartation thereof. After hearing the group's intent to visit and serve at Mother Teresa's Home for the Destitute and Dying, the businessman said with a smile on his face and a reverence in his voice, "Mother Teresa is the greatest Indian who ever lived."

I shook my head in agreement, but asked, "Even more than

- 108 -

Gandhi?"

"Even more than Gandhi!"

I've been to the grave of Gandhi and found it quite moving, for he was a hero to every loyal son and daughter of India. For this businessman to say what he said about Mother Teresa, exemplified the love that Muslims, Sikhs, Hindus and Christians alike possessed for this amazing woman.

In the years preceding September 11, 2001, Mother Teresa travelled the world over without a passport. The entire world knew who she was. She was invited to the greatest of palaces and mansions where she never slept in a bed, choosing, instead, to sleep on the ground as a way of identifying with the poor and needy. Many of her direct and pointed comments could easily have been judged politically incorrect, and yet Mother Teresa was flooded with invitations to presidential residences and prime ministers' chambers, and her advice on politics was solicited by many of the world's most powerful leaders. She was one of the most respected human beings who ever walked on planet earth and already beatified, it is widely agreed that it will only be a matter of time until the Roman Catholic Church canonizes her as a saint.

When the train finally arrived, the team proceeded to their designated positions and followed the directives they had been given the day before. They had been informed of the high danger potential in the city—the thefts, the brutality, the false imprisonments, etc., and they understood the importance of sticking together as a team. Everyone had a role to play. Some were responsible for transporting the luggage off the train and others were part of the group that formed a protective circle around the luggage outside the train.

These young people between the ages of fourteen and eighteen, operated as a harmonious team, following my instructions with absolute precision. They were in a situation where success would be determined by interdependence and they rose to the occasion. It was a sight to see!

We left the train and the tracks that were covered with all manner of waste and human feces and continued our walk down the main street toward the hostel. I could see the students soaking in the sights and the smells; every element of the experience. One student later confided in me that visiting India was like visiting another planet. Another student stated after the trip that the Indian people were the most beautiful people he had ever seen on planet earth. He thought that their dark skin and colorful attire created an exquisite and lovely picture.

As we walked down the busy street, we observed poverty everywhere, not dissimilar to what you've no doubt seen on film, television or in print. The only problem was that you couldn't change channels or turn pages to escape these disturbing images. People slept in the streets as beggars tenaciously plied their trade. The bazaar itself was an unending maze of narrow streets shared by pedestrians, cars, handcarts, man-drawn rickshaws, motorized rickshaws, scooters and cows each forcing their way through the crowd. This was accompanied by a surreal underscore of the incessant cacophony of hundreds, perhaps thousands of automobile horns.

Due to my own condition and fifteen of my students, one of our first challenges was to find a hospital where we could obtain medical help in fighting off fever and infection. Once there, for a grand total of forty dollars, each of us saw a doctor and received a thorough examination, along with a prescription for necessary antibiotics. We left the doctor's office and headed toward our rooms hoping to get some much needed rest.

Two days later, the team boarded a bus and drove to Mother Teresa's Home for the Destitute and Dying. I'll never forget the look on each team member's face as they walked through the doors and witnessed living skeletons staring at them with smiles on their faces and appreciation in their beautiful brown eyes. I was privileged to see both the girls and the boys on the team extend themselves to these dying patients. Many of the team members held grown Indian people in their arms and fed them bottles filled with liquid and medication. Each one of them served in some capacity at Mother Teresa's Home.

I especially remember watching sixteen year-old Amy as she held an old Indian woman in her arms and treated the woman with all the care and tenderness she would have given to her own mother. She cradled the weakened woman and lovingly stroked her hair as she fed her a bottle. It was emotionally moving.

On the bus ride back to the hostel, Amy declared that she had found her purpose in life. She expressed how she had never experienced such meaning as when she was holding the Indian woman in her arms.

Amy's words were especially poignant considering her background.

Like so many young people, Amy was the product of a dysfunctional family. Her father was a police officer whose schedule kept him away from home to the extent that he struggled to find a connection with his daughter. As a result, she rebelled against any effort on his part to exercise parental authority.

Her mother suffered from a mental disorder, so Amy was left largely on her own, with no adult supervision. This young girl was basically raising herself and growing into a troubled and selfish teenager. So when she expressed a newfound purpose in life, it was nothing short of miraculous.

Years later, I heard a story about Mother Teresa on public radio—a story I wish I had known and been able to pass on to my students prior to the India trip.

Mother Teresa, it was told, had received a letter from a person inquiring about purpose and happiness. After several months, she finally responded with a letter that contained four words: "Find your own Calcutta."

Mother Teresa later explained that finding your own Calcutta involved finding the sick, the suffering and the lonely right where you are—in your own homes and families, in your workplaces and schools. She wrote that one could find "Calcutta" all over the world, if they had the eyes to see. Everywhere we go, wherever we are, there are people who are unwanted, unloved, uncared for, rejected by society, completely forgotten, and completely left alone.

Mother Teresa was an exemplary model of giving her life away—a masterful teacher in every sense of the word. As an educator, I am reminded that I don't need to travel the world over to find the needy. We have needy students in our very own schools. Schools all around this great planet are "Calcuttas" for educators. Wherever we are, we must find our own "Calcutta."

8

"You Can"

TEACHER IN THE MIRROR

Can you imagine? Can you conceive of what might happen if you were released from the grip of fear and took a risk? What could happen if you began to give generously of your time, talent and treasure? What could happen to your gifting if you were daring enough? What might happen in your personal relationships if you allowed yourself to be vulnerable and transparent? Can you imagine the legacy you would leave for your students?

In chapter one I introduced you to my high school football coach who drilled into me that "can't" is a word that is foe to ambition. It spoke to me then, and it continues to speak to me today.

Over the years I have learned that the word "can," as opposed to "can't," is a word that says, "I will!" At the very least, the word "can" implies an attempt, an effort, an undertaking, a struggle and/or a venture. "Can't," simply declares, "I won't."

Many educators say, "I can't do this. I can't do that. I'm not talented enough, strong enough, disciplined enough or good enough." Many choose to say, "I can't start over or begin anew. I can't become that or accomplish this. I can't win the hearts and minds of students when I'm struggling with my own peace and well-being.

The word "can't" has inhibited vast numbers of people from being and becoming the people they were meant to be. It has kept so many teachers from fulfilling the dreams and purposes they have in their hearts.

A traditional fable records a tale about the tragedy of unrealized potential. In the story, the eagle did not believe he could fly, he did not see himself as the king of the birds—mighty, courageous and bold. Instead, this eagle was ignorant of his strength and unaware of his superior vision and powerful talons. He was an eagle who simply believed the "I can't" lies.

It all began one day when a farmer found an eagle's egg. He put it with his mother hens, and soon the egg hatched. The young eagle grew up with all the other chickens. Whatever the chickens did, the eagle also did. He thought he was a chicken, just like the birds surrounding him. Since the chickens could only fly for a short distance, the eagle also learned to fly only a short distance. He thought that was what he was supposed to do, so that was all that he thought he could do.

One day the eagle saw a bird flying high above him. He was very impressed.

"Who is that?" he asked the hens around him.

"That's the eagle, the king of the birds," the hens told him. "He belongs to the sky. We belong to the earth. We are chickens!"

So the eagle lived and died a chicken, for that's what he thought he was.

The metaphor is simple. Many have lived and died with unrealized power and purpose, much like the eagle in this fable.

It is true that chickens seldom fly. They are fat and lazy birds, content to live inside a fence, scratching around for grubs and worms—looking for the path of least resistance. Whenever a storm comes chickens choose to run to the shelter of the chicken coop and to the comfort of the other chickens.

Eagles, on the other hand, are strong and free. They often travel alone and distance themselves from the crowd. Eagles have great wisdom and vision. They dwell in the high places, build their nests on the rocks and are faithful, dependable mates. They are protective, caring parents and they have learned to soar high on powerful air currents.

My friend, we are not destined for a mediocre, mundane, chicken-type existence.

We, like eagles, are meant for greatness. We exist to soar and to live disciplined and brilliant lives without fear, failure or remorse.

Maybe you feel like the chicken, stuck in the barnyard, fenced in, living on the feed that is provided, and scratching out a daily humdrum existence.

Maybe you have found yourself vainly attempting to find your place in life's "pecking order." Or maybe the storms of life have caused you to simply give up on the belief that positive change is possible.

Maybe an "I can't" attitude has permeated your life.

Maybe the lack of passion reigns supreme and continues to wreak havoc on you mentally, physically and relationally.

In an age of self-indulgence, instant gratification, diversion and distraction, I make an appeal to each one of you: I challenge you to live a life of vitality, freedom, empowerment and love rather than defeat, slavery, secrecy and selfishness. You are called to something so much greater than mediocrity.

It takes a conscious decision to turn your "I can't" into "I can." For decades, teachers have read "The Little Engine That Could." The lessons of hard work and belief in oneself resonate in this beautiful children's story. If the Little Engine is going to make it up and over the high mountain, he's going to need an "I can" attitude. "I think I can… I think I can!" he tells himself. And, the little train repeats this mantra over and over again throughout the story until the seemingly impossible task becomes reality.

Being an educator, who wins the hearts and minds of young people, is really about having an "I can" attitude. No matter how big the obstacle, if you think you can—you can. Thinking you can, is the engine that will drive you to success.

I once had a friend tell me, "Scott, don't hold on to what you can't keep."

Educators who allow love to be their motivation, the engine that pulls their train, will live rich, full lives for they will have given away that which they can't keep. As I age and mature, I don't want to become cranky and critical. Rather, I want to be filled with love and a positive "I CAN" attitude.

Many years ago when I was beginning my teaching career, I

heard someone say: "No one gets rich teaching, but nobody lives a richer life."

Good things in life aren't measured in dollars. Chances are that the amount of money you have made, the size of your home, the model of car you drive, or any other material thing will not mark your passing. Rather, the only investment that will matter is your investment into the lives and relationships that surround you.

Remember—you can scratch with the chickens, or you can soar with the eagles. It's your choice.

Your students need you...your students are depending on you. So, be a hero!

Win their hearts...win their minds!

BIOGRAPHY

Scott Braden has been in the educational trenches for twenty years. He is credentialed in the State of California as a public school teacher and a public school administrator. Scott also has postgraduate degrees in History and Educational Leadership. He currently is a secondary principal and resides in Visalia, California. He is married to Cheryl Braden and together they have two children—Hannah and Micah.

Having traveled nationally and internationally as a motivational and inspirational speaker, Scott's greatest joy is inspiring people to find purpose, life and vitality.

End Notes

a   http://thinkexist.com/quotes/horace_mann/

b   Dr. Spencer Kagan and Miguel Kagan, Kagan Cooperative Learning: 2009 Kagan Publishing (San Clemente, California): 2.4:2.15

c   http://www.cde.ca.gov/eo/in/se/charactered.asp

d   http://www.physicsforums.com/archive/index.php/t-17068. html

e   http://thinkexist.com/quotation/dont_ask_what_the_world_needs-ask_what_makes_you/346829.html